Also by Bill O'Reilly

The O'Reilly Factor:
The Good, the Bad, and the Completely
Ridiculous in American Life

The No Spin Zone:
Confrontations with the Powerful
and Famous in America

Who's Looking Out for You?

Those Who Trespass: A Novel

Bill O'Reilly

and Charles Flowers

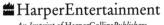 HarperEntertainment
An Imprint of HarperCollins*Publishers*

THE O'REILLY FACTOR for Kids

A SURVIVAL
GUIDE FOR
AMERICA'S
FAMILIES

HarperCollins books may be purchased for educational, business, or sales promotional use. For information please write: Special Markets Department, HarperCollins Publishers Inc., 10 East 53rd Street, New York, NY 10022.

FIRST EDITION

Printed on acid-free paper

Library of Congress Cataloging-in-Publication Data

O'Reilly, Bill.
    The O'Reilly factor for kids: a survival guide for America's families / by Bill O'Reilly and Charles Flowers.
        p. cm.
    ISBN 0-06-054424-4
    1. Youth—Life skills guides. 2. Youth—Conduct of life. 3. Interpersonal relations in adolescence. 4. Adolescent psychology. I. Flowers, Charles. II. Title.

HQ796.O655 2004
646.7'00835—dc22
                                                                2004047266

04   05   06   07   08   WBC/RRD   20 19 18 17 16 15 14 13 12 11

This book is for Madeline and Spencer O'Reilly. Constantly, you are loved.

—B.O'R.

For the late Professor Joe Summers, whose every word and gesture was an act of teaching.

—C.F.

CONTENTS

Contents

ACKNOWLEDGMENTS

Charles Flowers and I worked on this book intensely.
Makeda Wubneh provided her usual brilliant assistance,
and our editors at HarperCollins, Hope Innelli and
Jeffery McGraw, helped immensely. Also, the hundreds
of American kids who wrote to us were a source of great
inspiration.

—B.O'R.

My thanks to the many kids, parents, teachers, and
school psychologists who kept Bill and me current,
especially Helen Rollo, Nina Weinberg, Jean McGlinn,
Penny Constantine, Suzé Leshin, J. Lloyd Jacobs, and
Tony Sabella. And I'm grateful for the privilege and
fun of learning so much from my former students at
Catalina Island School, Palmdale High School, Fremont
High School, and the University of Rochester.

—C.F.

EYEWITNESS REPORT

I am 15½ years old. You said on your show, Mr. O'Reilly, for kids aged 10 to 16 to write in about the biggest problem in their life. Well, the biggest problem in my life is actually the future. I worry about getting married and having babies, and graduating high school, and if I'm going to college or not, and just handling the stress of growing up, period. Peer pressure . . . These emotions I feel for no reason . . . Boys . . . you know? Stuff like that. Well, that's the biggest problem in my life. Just kind of growing up and feeling that pressure, you know. It's scary.

—*Elizabeth in Ohio*

DIRECT TO YOU FROM BILL O'REILLY

I wish I'd had this book when I was a teenager because, like Elizabeth, I had many concerns.

Unfortunately, no one had written a realistic book for kids. So I made dumb mistakes, got in trouble because I was too stubborn to know better, and did things I wish I could forget.

I'm going to tell you about some of those things in this book. Maybe you'll laugh at my boneheaded behavior, but that's okay, as long as you end up smarter than I was at your age.

The O'Reilly Factor for Kids is a survival guide. It will give you an edge in facing the challenges of this crazy but exciting time of your life. And that edge will make your life easier.

What does an adult know? Well, I have a career that's lots of fun and makes me a lot of money. I've also never forgotten what it was like to be a teenager. No one does.

You may have seen me on my daily TV program, *The O'Reilly Factor,* or heard me on the radio. If you have, you know that I tell it straight, no matter what. And I make sure my guests tell the truth, too. (Telling yourself the truth is going to be one of the hardest jobs in your teen years. I'll show you how.)

I am as honest in this guide as I am on the air. No sugarcoating. This is straight stuff.

At this stage of my life, I know who I am and, best of all, I know how to choose friends I can trust and stay away from people who are poison. I want you to have the same kind of knowledge, and I want you to have it now so you can get on top of life earlier than I did.

I spent years making stupid decisions, even in adult life, but somehow I made it through all the mistakes. Now I know that even though I have achieved success, I could have done much better along the way. I'm determined to show you how.

But *The O'Reilly Factor for Kids* is not about me. This book is about *you*. About finding the courage and willpower to be who you really are. About standing up for yourself. About doing the smartest thing.

Did you notice what I said? "The smartest thing." This guide is not necessarily about what's right and what's wrong. It's about using your head.

Listen up . . .

PEOPLE IN
Your Life

EYEWITNESS REPORT

I've lost one of my best friends . . . She meant everything to me . . . I feel as if I'm missing a part of myself without her.

—*Melissa in Tennessee*

I'm a 15-year-old high school student who is quite happy with my life except for the fights that my friends get me into.

—*Sara in Ohio*

I like to play softball, and the only problem is boys. They can be so irritating, and yet so interesting.

—*Deanna in California*

My biggest problem is girls. They are, oh, so confusing.

—*Eric in Tennessee*

FRIENDS

lmost everybody watched the TV show *Friends* on NBC. Unfortunately, some kids think that's what real friends are like. Of course, we can learn a lot of things from our *Friends* on television, but sitcoms are very different from real life.

In real life, true friends stand by you when things get rough. If you get sick or have a tragedy in your family, your real friends will be there to listen and to help. Sure, they do that in the TV program, but the tragedies those characters experience last only twenty-three minutes. Yours will last much longer, so your friends will have to last much longer, too.

TV friends are also always fooling around. You can't do that in real life. There will be times when you will have to do some very difficult things. If you have friends who will help you, you'll be a lot better off.

My Story:

I once had a friend in high school whom I confided in. This guy and I had known each other since first grade and we were pretty solid. At least, I thought we were. Freshman year is always tough because you are the youngest in the school and are still trying to figure out the program. There was this dance I wanted to go to, but I didn't want to go alone. I wanted some guys to hang with so the girls would think I was cool. So I asked my friend, who was usually up for this kind of thing, if he would come along. He said he couldn't go. I said fine and found a couple of other guys to go with me. But when we arrived at the hop (that's what they called a dance back then), I couldn't believe my eyes. My so-called friend who told me he couldn't go to the dance was out there doing the twist like a madman. What was up with that? I cornered this so-called friend later, and he admitted that some of the guys he went to the dance with didn't like me, so he didn't want me around.

If that situation had happened in a TV sitcom, everybody would have made up and had a few laughs. But life is different. I never trusted that guy again and rarely spoke to him. Since he never apologized, I think I made the smart decision. He wasn't a true friend, and that happens a lot in life. By not wasting any more time with him, I went on to make real friends, many of whom I hang around with to this day. I'm that kind of guy: once I become friends with you, I'm in for life unless you do something bad to me. Even though I am now famous and successful, I still keep my old friends. And believe me, none of them looks like Jennifer Aniston. It would not be hard being *her* friend.

Okay, you know I've made money. It was a long time coming, so I don't usually spend much of it and I certainly don't show it off.

(We're going to talk about money smarts later in this book.) But one thing I do that costs a few bucks is set up a trip every year to some exotic faraway place—the Caribbean, the Hawaiian Islands—where I sail and swim and dive with old friends.

And I do mean "old friends." I've known some of these guys since we were four years old, others from high school and college, and still others from my early years in television. I've been lucky to have such friends, but I've also worked hard at it. We trust one another. We care about one another's families. We laugh a lot. We remember a lot.

I hope you can have such friends when you're my age.

Of course, you can't control all of the circumstances that help friendships develop and last. I grew up in the same house until I went away to college. The kids in my neighborhood really knew one another. We went to the same schools, terrorized the same teachers, dated the same girls.

Now, I don't want you to think that I sat around when I was your age and carefully chose my companions because of their virtues. No way. I ran with the loudmouthed, brash, unruly kids. We looked like bums; we acted like maniacs. We did very stupid things.

But even though we would not have used these words back then, we were loyal to one another. One for all, all for one: we really were like that.

And because I had experienced true friendship, which grew over the years through many different situations (not all of them fun, by any means), I got very, very spoiled. I mean, throughout the rest of my life, I have expected new friends to be as honest and loyal as my old friends.

Is that stupid?

Maybe. But that's the way I am.

Other people will tell you to forgive a friend for lying to you. Not me. Others will say that it is "mature" to expect your friends to have faults. Agreed. They can have all kinds of faults except dishonesty and disloyalty. Either of those is poison to a friendship. Sorry, but I can't see it any other way. Someone can lie to me once, but only once, if he or she wants to be a friend.

See, you heard I could be stubborn.

And I want you to be the same way, at least on this subject. You deserve friendship with people who can be trusted. You don't need to accept a so-called friendship with someone because he or she is "popular" or good-looking. None of that matters. I am surrounded in television by people who choose "friends" because they're rich or famous or sexy. That kind of friendship is called "groveling." And it lasts, such as it is, only as long as the other person has money, gets recognized on the street, or looks good in lowriders.

Everybody needs friends, but it's important you understand that not everybody can be a friend. Some kids are so selfish and insecure that no matter how nice you are to them, they will turn out to be untrustworthy. Don't blame yourself when a person you thought was your friend burns you. That happens a lot in life; the trick is to recognize and steer clear of those people who are messed up. I was always pretty good at selecting friends, but, as I mentioned, I've been betrayed as well.

There are some things that should tip you off right away that some kid you know is trouble. Violent behavior, for example, is a sure sign. If you know a kid who likes to physically hurt other people, get away from that person fast.

Same thing with someone who engages in malicious gossip. If somebody is constantly spreading dirt about other people, they'll do it to you, too.

If a kid lies to his parents, he or she will lie to you.

If a classmate cheats in school, he or she will cheat you.

If somebody borrows money and doesn't pay it back, drop that person as a friend.

If a kid flirts with your girlfriend or boyfriend, he or she is not your friend.

The list goes on and on. The important thing is to keep your eyes open. Bad behavior is seldom a onetime occurrence. Everybody makes mistakes, but if a kid is constantly doing rude or dishonest things, that kid is trouble. You do not need trouble.

One last tip: anyone who offers you drugs or alcohol is *definitely* not your friend. That is rule number one in life. Anybody who tempts you with stuff that can screw you up is a bad person. Get away, and stay away!

Some of you, I'm sad to say, may have parents who think it's a good idea to suck up to the rich kids or the smart kids in your school or neighborhood. This time they're wrong. If you try building friendships now for the wrong reasons, you'll be lost for the rest of your life.

By the way, it works both ways. No one should want to be your friend unless you're ready to be honest and loyal, too.

"Keep your friendships in repair," warned Ralph Waldo Emerson (and if you haven't heard of him, look him up). In other words, friendship takes a lot of work. Sometimes a good friend is boring, just as you can be, too. Sometimes a good friend does something stupid. But as I said before, you can endure faults in a friend as long as he or she's loyal and honest.

Here's the O'Reilly List of True Friendship Factors:

1. DON'T LIE.
2. BE THERE IN THE BAD TIMES.
3. BE FREE WITH COMPLIMENTS.
4. NOTICE WHEN SOMETHING'S WRONG.
5. KNOW WHEN TO LISTEN.
6. KNOW WHEN TO INTERVENE.
7. BE YOURSELF.
8. LET YOUR FRIEND BE HIMSELF.
9. LAUGH A LOT.

My Story:

Growing up on Long Island just a few miles outside New York City, I had tons of friends in the neighborhood. They were all guys, because at that time women's lib had not kicked in and the girls played differently than we did. Forty years later, I still have many of those friends, if you can believe it. We've stayed in touch because we formed such a strong bond way back then.

In all that time I can't remember any of my friends ever asking me to do anything that was truly awful. Yeah, when we were young we smoked some cigarettes and knocked over some garbage cans at night. But our pranks were harmless and usually so dopey we wound up laughing at ourselves.

When I was four years old, I met Lenny. He was kind of a slow kid, but I didn't care. He lived close by, so we played together with two other kids, Gene and Kenny. As we got older, Lenny began to drift apart from us. He didn't like sports, and he wasn't very outgoing. Ten years later, Lenny still lived in the neighborhood but had stopped talking to all of his old friends. He had new friends, but we knew they were bad news. Lenny and his new pals looked down on us because they thought we were uncool.

Even then, I knew Lenny was heading for big trouble. He became a drug addict and died of AIDS before he was forty years old. (Hint: That's not old.) His new friends also made disasters of their lives. And there was nothing my friends and I could do about it. Lenny made the decision to walk away from the neighborhood kids who accepted him to hang out with kids who were screwed up.

Next time some kid tries to convince you to do something you know is wrong, think of Lenny. And also think of his mother. He broke her heart.

A few of my other friends also fell into destructive habits—and they all paid a price, too. If you choose the road of getting high, committing crimes, disrespecting others, or engaging in violence, you will make a mess of your life. Nobody who does these things escapes the fall. Nobody.

Like many things we'll talk about, learning to develop true friendships now is training for a happy, successful, richly rewarding adult life. Sure, it's exciting to meet the many powerful and famous people who appear on my television and radio programs. But they're not friends. Some of the saddest occasions you can imagine are parties in New York and Hollywood where everybody is famous and wants to be seen, but no one is there to enjoy and develop friendships.

Friends are there when you need them, just as you must be there when they need you.

Friends do not share your secrets with other people. Friends know the worst things about you, and love you anyway. They know the best things about you, and respect them.

EYEWITNESS REPORT

They call me "mole," "neuter," and other rude names in middle school. Once it got so bad that my teacher called my house. People should treat others the way they want to be treated.

—*Christina in California*

My worst problem is the bullies in school. They are definitely going to get a call from the ACLU in their later life.

—*Ian in Kansas*

I'm constantly called "gay" because I don't fit in with the "in crowd," and I don't want to, because I like to stay out of trouble. I'm constantly harassed, and sometimes I actually get punched in the face or hit in the stomach with a textbook. I've tried to do everything to stop this, but nothing works. I feel like one of those people out of a movie that is the one that is picked on.

—*Aaron in Tennessee*

I'm diabetic, and I'm fine with it, but some kids make fun of me. I've tried everything, but they don't stop.

—*Mindy in Georgia*

These two girls who are a year older than me (I'm in 4th grade) bully me on the bus. They make fun of me. They call me words I don't know. They say I'm unintelligent, meaningless, hopeless, and helpless . . . I wish they never existed. I don't know what to do.

—*Joe*

BULLIES

Bullies are cowards.

I know, because I fought them, but I'll tell you that story a little later.

This chapter is for anyone who is being bullied, but it's also for the fools who *are* bullies. And it's for everyone else, too, because bullying can muck up your playground, your class, your life!

This isn't a small problem. According to a report by the National Association of School Psychologists cited in William S. Pollock's fine book about teenage boys, *Real Boys' Voices,* an estimated 160,000 kids stay home from school every day in America because they're afraid of being bullied. If it hasn't happened to you, you're lucky. If it has, you know the kind of hell they're going through.

And that hell does not have to be physical. When a group of girls ignores another girl they think is dorky, or doesn't ever let her sit with them at lunch, or giggles about her hair or clothing or acne, that can be a form of psychological bullying. We're social animals. Few things are more frightening than being purposely excluded from a group. Whenever a group is cruel to an outsider, the mental scars can be permanent.

Sometimes other people notice bullying, but there are times when it's harder to spot, because some of the cruelest bullying does not involve physical abuse. Instead some bullies use a more subtle form of alienation to hurt their targets. Generally, bullies pick on people who are smaller or perceived to be weaker or "different." Why? Because misery loves company. Most times, bullies don't like something about themselves, so they try to make others feel as bad about themselves as the bully feels about himself. In many cases, making someone else feel weak makes a bully feel strong.

Think of the bullies you've met. Are they the best athletes, the sharpest students, the most popular classmates? Never. Those cool people don't need to belittle others. They know that they're worth something, are admired, and are succeeding. No. Bullies are losers. They don't have true friends to keep them straight. Often they're out of shape, awkward physically, or can't afford new or stylish clothes. They're not happy or busy with school and social activities. They're lonely and angry people.

So what should you and everybody else do about them?

In a perfect world, all bullies would read this, see how stupid their behavior is, wise up—and stop hurting people.

But as you are finding out in many ways at your age, this is not a perfect world. This problem has to be handled by the victim, and fear can make that a very difficult thing to do.

My dad, who was a large, tough Irishman, would have given me simple advice if he knew a bully was bothering me: "Deck him!" But I was always a big kid, played sports well, and had a loyal set of friends. I was also never afraid to fight, so I wasn't exactly the kind of target bullies usually picked on. But despite all that, I got bullied in high school once, too . . .

My Story:

I attended a private school on Long Island where there were plenty of rich kids in my class. I was not a rich kid. Maybe you are in the same situation. You know other kids with lots of money and expensive clothes and all the latest gadgets. But your money is limited and there's no way your parents are going to buy you expensive stuff. If you are in this position, know that most American kids are like you. Later in life you will appreciate what you are able to achieve and acquire far more than some spoiled person who has had everything given to him.

Anyway, we had to wear jackets and ties in my high school, and my jackets were cheap pieces of junk. Also, my tie was a clip-on, since I couldn't care less about ties and didn't want to learn how to knot the dumb things. So a few wise guys started teasing me about my clothes. One of them even pulled my tie off. I gave that guy a shove and warned him that bad things would happen if he continued down this particular road.

But the hazing didn't stop there. In fact, it went on for months, and believe me, it was annoying. Still, I didn't say anything to the teachers or my parents. I toughed it out. Then one day two clowns cornered me at my locker and grabbed my jacket, mocking me. Without hesitation, I decked one of them with a couple of punches and the other guy ran. One of the teachers witnessed the fight and I got into trouble. I couldn't believe it. I told the teacher what happened, but he didn't much care. So I took the fall and had to do detention after school.

That night at home I went ballistic, and for once my father actually listened to my rantings. He told me to cool off and said he'd take care of things.

The next day my detention was canceled and all of a sudden

nobody was bothering me. I don't know what exactly my father said or did, but apparently he solved the problem. After that, the bullying stopped almost completely.

The lesson here is to confide in your parents or a teacher you believe is fair. It is dumb to think you're squealing, because bullying is inexcusable and no kid should have to put up with it. If you happen to have parents who are not very approachable or are not particularly good at handling these types of situations, know that there are usually adults in a position of authority at school who can and will intervene for you if you ask them to.

Before doing that, however, you might want to try one last thing. If the bully isn't a complete jerk, talking can sometimes work. Saying something like this might help: "Why bother me? I haven't done anything to you. We're on the same bus every day, so let's work this out."

Occasionally, but not all of the time, eye-to-eye contact and a simple, straightforward confrontation will put a stop to the bullying. I'm serious. Sometimes, but certainly not all of the time, the bully will actually become a friend. I've seen that happen a few times because it turned out that the bully, in a very stupid way, was just trying to get attention.

You might also try changing your daily pattern to avoid the bully. If he corners you at lunch, make sure you eat with a group of friends. If she follows you home, get involved in some activity that keeps you at school longer (provided there are still other people around after school), or make plans to go shopping with someone. If the bully has to work to keep up with you, he may just give up.

But if the situation is really tough, you should turn to the right adults for help. Of course, your parents will be concerned, but because they are not as close to the situation as a teacher or counselor at school, you might want to discuss the problem with a school official, too. Ask for advice, then try to act on that advice by yourself.

If that doesn't work, adults will have to step in. There is no shame in this. Here's what I did . . .

My Story:

After my father calmed the bullies down, I did not say a word about what happened. I figured that what my father did was nobody's business, including my own. I never once asked him what happened. But I did tell him that things were a lot better and thanked him for his help. I know my dad appreciated that—and the fact that I didn't fall apart under pressure.

Also, I never mentioned anything to the bullies themselves because I wanted to let the whole deal die down. But I did keep an eye on those guys to see if they were torturing other kids. I wasn't going to let that happen, either.

By the way, you don't have to be the one who is being bullied to speak up. If you're observing a bullying situation from the outside, you should be just as concerned. Do you know what all of the school shooting episodes you have heard about in the news have in common? In each case, a kid or group of kids who felt rejected or bullied by others finally had enough and came to school with their guns blazing. So if you see a bully in action, tell someone in authority whom you trust. You may actually help save kids' lives or at the very least make the life of the kid who is being bullied a whole lot better.

Admittedly, there were occasions when I gave other kids a hard time myself . . .

My Story:

As for Bill O'Reilly the Bully, it was a onetime episode. I played Little League baseball with a group of neighborhood guys. We all resented this one kid because his father always came to games and made sure that he played a lot, even though he wasn't very good. One night, when his father wasn't around, we began calling him names. I was the loudest and rudest of all. Suddenly, the father, his face red with fury, came running down the street toward us. I split.

But the old man was fast. I raced into my house and up the stairs. I couldn't believe it—he was right behind me. He stopped in the living room where my father, the tough, large Irishman, was staring in astonishment. I didn't hear the conversation, but I expected to be confronted by my father later. He never hesitated to use physical punishment when he thought I had behaved badly.

But this time he did something unexpected, and it cured my stupid behavior. He came into my bedroom. He didn't hit me. He simply said, very calmly, "The boy's father is not quite right in the head. So he's got enough problems, okay? Lay off him." No, I didn't befriend the guy, but I shut up. I realized that I was teasing someone who had a tough situation at home that I couldn't even begin to understand.

My father shamed me, and I got the message: No one should bully anyone, and no one should have to suffer through it, either.

Speak up, and stop the madness.
Nobody has the right to make you unhappy!

EYEWITNESS REPORT

The biggest problem in my life right now is arguing with my mom. She won't let me wear what I want to wear. She won't let me call my boyfriends. I still love her and all, but you see she's really, really annoying me.

—*Kayla in Colorado*

My mother nags me about almost everything, and my father is insecure about me driving. It's just plain hard being a teenager.

—*Jami in Ohio*

If my parents are not arguing with me, they are arguing with each other! I'd rather them yell at me than have them yelling at each other right in front of me.

—*Alex in Pennsylvania*

My parents want to know every little detail about my life, and since I wouldn't tell them, they're sending me to a "family counselor." I HATE IT!

—*Pesh*

PARENTS

Are they always right?

No. They're human, and they come in all different types.

Let's be clear. Most of our parents are exactly what we need. In some cases, though, parents are not capable, loving, or sensible enough. In fact, there are even a few parents out there who are downright toxic. But I'll get to all that in a minute. I just want you to know up front that I know it's not always "You're wrong, they're right!"

Now that we got that established, let's discuss something that's probably been happening to you a lot these days. One of the most important things about the teen years is that you begin to look outside yourself and evaluate other people. Maybe the reason for doing this is a little bit selfish: you want to understand what other kids are like so that you can make them like you better. Fine. But while you're working on that, you should also be learning how other people think and feel. Essentially what you are doing is learning *empathy*.

You're discovering (I hope) that you can't understand someone else's behavior unless you try to understand what they're going through. If your girlfriend curses at you, you'll want to know why she's so upset. Has she just suffered some kind of disappointment? And girls, it's the same thing with guys. You can really drive them crazy. But why? When that happens, you really want to know the answer to that question.

The same should be true for your relationship with your parents. You should be learning to use this kind of thinking, this same empathy, on them, all the while remembering that they have the ultimate say.

You and your folks might have conflicting aims. You want a new bike, but your parent says no. If you're still a child, you just get angry or sad. But if you're a teenager, you're just learning to ask yourself why. Is your mother worried because some kid across town just got killed when his Harley slammed into a tree? Is your father concerned because he might lose his job and he needs to keep as much money as possible in reserve? Would your bike make insurance costs too high for the family?

Even if this scenario has nothing to do with you, I know that you can come up with one on your own that is relevant to your life.

The example doesn't matter. Here's what does:

1. **IN EVERY ARGUMENT, YOU SHOULD BEGIN BY ISOLATING THE CONFLICT.** What are you and your parents really disagreeing about?

2. **DO NOT BRING UP ISSUES OF RIGHT AND WRONG.** Are your parents wrong? According to you, yes. According to them, no. So there's no going there. You KNOW that you're right, of course.

3. **INSTEAD, FIND OUT WHY THEY DISAGREE WITH YOU.** If your father says, "Because I said so," this strategy might not be working. But keep cool and try again. You might be surprised. The more polite you are, the more responsive the other person will be. Remember that in any debate.

4. **ONCE YOU UNDERSTAND THEIR REASON(S), SEE WHAT YOU CAN WORK OUT.** Safety concerns? Offer to take a safe driving course. Money? Find a job, or go for the secondhand option.

5. **BUT IF NOTHING WORKS . . . DROP IT.** This is an important life lesson. Sometimes all of the rationality in the world will still not be enough to change the mind of someone close to you. This lesson is important in marriage and business partnerships, too, so you might as well learn it now by dealing with your parents. Even if they are being unfair, remember that life is unfair.

I did not learn this lesson when I was a teenager . . .

My Story:

During my junior year in high school I made the ice hockey team and was the starting goalie. But there was one problem: I didn't have enough money for the goaltending equipment, which can be quite expensive. So I got creative. I used my baseball glove with a pad sewn onto the bottom of it, a baseball catcher's chest protector I borrowed from a friend, a lacrosse mask I found at some rummage sale, and old skates. But I absolutely had to have the heavy goalie leg pads because those pucks can break bones. I found some thirdhand ones for twenty bucks, which I earned by babysitting.

I have to admit I was a bit teed off at my parents because everybody else had brand-new equipment. But, again, I didn't have any choice. Either I played with what I had, or I didn't play at all. So I skated out there and did pretty well. I used my anger about not having good equipment to help block every puck that came at me. By the way, that's another O'Reilly tip—it's okay to get angry about stuff, but channel that anger so that it helps you. I could have quit the team and moped around, but what good would that have done? That's just not smart. Instead, I had a great time, and my team made the playoffs.

Yes, I still resented my parents for a long time because they didn't supply me with what some other kids had . . . but you have the chance to be smarter than I was.

As I've already said, life is not fair. Learn this now!

And that means you will not get everything you want in life. You can take that as a negative, or you can look for the positive in that truth. Your parents may disagree with you on some issue, but when you open your mind and figure out why, you will be more mature and will also understand how lucky you are. Their motives have to do with their love for you, with their concern for keeping the family stable, with the hard work they're doing to make your life comfortable.

You think you want parents who give you everything you want? But you're wrong. Those parents are not preparing you for life. Unless they are going to stand beside you, handing you money, as you go out in the world, buy a house, and raise your own family, they will be giving you a dangerously false impression of your future.

Finally, as I suggested earlier, there are a few parents out there who are truly toxic. They are people with emotional problems, or people who are prisoners of addiction, unable to empathize with you or anyone else.

If you are a child of that type of parent, you have it tough, and I feel for you. But you can't give up. You must learn how to find adults—relatives, teachers, counselors, coaches, or neighbors—who are good people and can give you good advice when you need it. You will also have to find friends who are mature enough to help you through bad times.

If you have younger sisters and brothers, you have the responsibility of looking out for them, too.

And as long as your parents are not abusing you or others around you, you should do your best—difficult as it is—to stay with your family until you get a good education and can make it on your own.

These are guidelines, not a solution. I know that I can't tell you in a few sentences how to deal with a home life made unhappy by bad parenting. What I can tell you, for what it's worth, is that some of the strongest, kindest adults I know have made their way upward from very bad family situations.

But I was more fortunate, and so are most teenagers. Every teen gets frustrated with his or her parents, but if you try to empathize, you are likely to have a better appreciation of them. After all, they've made you the center of their lives since you were born.

And one more thing (with me, there's always one more thing): you guys and gals aren't all that smart yet. Whether you believe me now or not, your parents know more than you do, so accept it.

My father forced me to wear braces on my teeth. I hated them and him (at the time) for making me go through that ordeal. But I was a jerk! Those braces made my later teen years and adulthood a lot easier. And you don't see many people on TV with bad teeth!

Figure it out: you are not smarter than the adults in your life. Someday you may well surpass them. But not now. No way. Accept it.

EYEWITNESS REPORT

My brother is in Mosul, Iraq. I miss him a lot and I wish that he would come home soon . . . It is a lot different with somebody you know and love being over there. The only thing I want is for him to be safe so that he can come home and give me a big hug and we would be all right.

—*Katie in Wisconsin*

My big sister is mean to me, and when I get a friend she just takes it away from me and well, Bill, you would not want her to be your sister, okay?

—*Jamie in Arizona*

I worry about the war and how long it will go on, and if my brother will have to go if they start the draft.

—*Alec in Oklahoma*

SIBLINGS:
your BROTHER,
your SISTER

I remember well when my young daughter met one of her life-long best friends.

It happened at the hospital when she saw her baby brother for the first time. Of course, she didn't know right then what her mother and I knew from our own experiences: there will be tussles and arguments and even physical fights, but in the long run your brothers and sisters will be there for you. At least, I hope so.

If you're lucky, you know that already. But it's also possible—and very, very normal—that you and a sibling think you CAN'T STAND each other and that you never will! She's selfish! He's mean! She makes fun of you in front of her snooty friends! He embarrasses you by acting like a three-year-old in front of your girlfriend!

Okay, if none of this sounds familiar to you, you may want to skip to the next chapter.

Still here?

Good. First of all, you need to know that conflict between siblings is bred into our genes. Think of birds in a nest squabbling over a nice juicy worm. You and your siblings are just like them. You are competing for what your family has to offer: the love of your parents, the food on the table, the money that can buy new clothes, toys and gadgets, the car that can free you for the evening . . . all of that and more. Even when there's more than enough to go around, it's somehow natural to try to get as much as you can.

But you can't have it all. That's natural, too. You're only one of the nestlings in your particular nest. You have to learn—and believe me, I know how awful these words can be when you want something—to share.

My Story:

I have a confession to make.

I was not always a good brother. My sister is two years younger than I am. When we were growing up I didn't help her out very much.

It's not as if I had to share much, because my interests and toys were so different from hers. But I could have been nicer. I could have shared some of my time. Unfortunately, I wasn't really thinking about her and her feelings. I remember my father yelling, "Be nice to your sister!" But I didn't listen.

I regret that now. Growing up, I missed out on my sister's life because I was so busy doing my own thing that I didn't really take the time to get to know her. I was selfish. I was dumb.

Today, my sister and I are friends. But I'll always look back and be disappointed by the way I treated her when she was little. So if you are giving your brothers and sisters a hard time, think about it. Someday, like me, you'll realize that it's uncool to treat your siblings poorly.

When you were a child, one of your parents' most difficult jobs—perhaps the most difficult job—was teaching you and your siblings to get along with one another. Now that you're in your teen years, you might want to use some of their tricks to avoid and resolve conflicts on your own.

For example, do you recall how your parents handled it when the childish you insisted on watching your favorite TV program even when dinner was ready or your siblings wanted to watch something else?

How did your mom react when the childish you insisted on playing with a sibling's friends even though they wanted to do something together on their own?

What did your dad do when the childish you pushed a sister down in the mud or teased your brother by calling him names?

If your parents handled such incidents with humor, tact, firmness, and reason, you have good role models for your behavior now. If a sibling is annoying you or getting in your space or monopolizing the computer, step back . . . think about what's really going on (is it that whole nestling-with-the-worm thing again?) . . . then figure out how to negotiate the problem from there.

"But that's unfair!" you say. "Why should I have to negotiate what's rightfully mine?"

I'll tell you why:

1. If you get good at this, you'll encounter **FEWER HASSLES IN THE FUTURE.**
2. **YOUR SIBLINGS WILL CATCH ON** (oh, yes, they will) and eventually they'll learn to return the favor.
3. **YOU WON'T DRIVE YOUR PARENTS CRAZY** . . . which can be good for everyone in the nest.
4. **YOU'LL BE LEARNING A LESSON** that can be used in many other areas of your life.
5. **IT'S THE SMART THING TO DO.**

Of the many things you will have to get good at as you mature, dealing with sibling conflict is one of the most important.

Once again, I'm talking about using your head. Why is a sibling acting "mean" or "childish" or in some other way you dislike? Does she think you get more attention from your parents? Does he think you have more friends at school? There's always a reason for annoying behavior. We just have to look beneath the surface to find it.

And while you're looking for that reason, you might also want to consider the age thing. Each position in the family order has different privileges and drawbacks. Think about it. Usually the eldest sibling appears to have the most freedom and the most responsibilities. You may resent an older sister for being allowed to stay out later at night than you, but do you know how often she babysat for you when you were an infant? Your older brother gets to drive the car, but doesn't that include taking time to pick you up from school or a friend's house?

Your youngest sibling may get more attention as the baby in the family, but she needs it because she *is* the youngest. As someone older now, you get to teach your younger sibling things, show her what you've learned, protect her from harm. If you've got your head on straight, you'll recognize this as a privilege, not a burden.

Of course, I don't know exactly what your family situation is. Let's be honest: your parents might handle brother–sister conflicts well, or they might fail all too often. Your siblings might respond to reasonable negotiation, or they might be total jerks. In any event, it's always best to try to resolve conflicts, establish boundaries, and encourage everyone to get along. But I also know that there are times when you can't do it all by yourself. You can only do your best, and if that fails, then perhaps the smartest thing to do is to just walk away.

But remember, even then there is hope for the future. When you and your siblings are out of that competitive nest and are trying to make it in the world outside, you'll have years of shared experience to draw upon. You'll forget the struggles and remember the good times. It's true. You'll get together to celebrate family joys and to comfort each other in times of tragedy. You'll share the challenges of taking care of your aging parents, the delight of watching the next generation grow up, and many more.

That all sounds very far away, I know, and maybe it even sounds unlikely to you right now. But here's one clue, I hope, that proves this is true. Look at the behavior of your parents and your aunts and uncles today. If they get along well, tell family jokes (over and over!), and help each other out, that is very likely what the future holds for you and your siblings.

And if your parents and their siblings don't enjoy one another's company in this way, then now is the time to try to build a better future for you and your siblings. One day they will be your "next of kin." And that's a powerful thing. All of us need to make the most of those ties.

EYEWITNESS REPORT

It's really idiotic, but I can't keep all of my friends happy by doing one thing, or acting one certain way. I can't keep my siblings happy, because I can't decide who to side with. I can't keep my parents or grandparents happy, either, just because they prefer to ignore me when I really want to be heard. It's hard to do everything that I have to do, and I procrastinate, and anger people because of it. I'm damned if I do something, and I'm damned if I don't!

—*Simone in Pennsylvania*

My biggest problem is my friends/boyfriends. I have four best friends, but keeping them happy, not getting in fights, and them giving me space is a lot to do. I've known them since birth, but it is very hard to keep things together.

—*Madeline in California*

STRIKING A
COMPROMISE

A ccording to my staff and friends, strangers always ask the same question about me: "Is he always like that?"

I suppose what they mean is, "Does he always act in real life the way he does on TV?"

Of course not.

I'm a straight talker, but I never waste my words on foolish people or idle chatter. I don't interrupt in social situations, unless it is absolutely necessary—that is, when somebody is lying or spreading malicious gossip.

The O'Reilly you see on TV is a man doing a job. I believe everything I say. I am trying to get powerful people to tell you the truth. I argue strongly and, I hope, clearly to get a story across.

Off-camera, after many years of not having good sense, I have learned a valuable lesson: life goes much more smoothly when you learn to compromise.

I'm not talking about compromising your values, your beliefs, or your goals. You have to stick firmly by those things or you're a weasel.

I'm talking about recognizing that other people in your life have just as much right to their ways of doing things as you do.

I'm talking about learning to choose which disagreements are important and which can be settled by compromise.

My Story:

W e all have things that we don't like to share, but if you force yourself to be generous, you will become a very popular kid.

And I'm not simply talking about stuff, either. It's important that you insist that everyone around you is treated fairly. Let's say that your friends are arguing over which movie to see. Nobody wants to compromise. Well, one solution might be to treat the discussion like a contest. One of you hides something . . . The first person to find it gets his or her movie choice.

That's called creative problem-solving. Nobody really likes to compromise, but the people who learn how to do it effectively are admired. And the kids who can make compromise fun . . . become legends!

If your parents haven't tried to teach you to compromise yet, they're doing you a real disservice.

Some of the saddest people I know were spoiled by their parents, then were amazed and overwhelmed when they had to face the real world. It's hard to make friends when you demand your way all the time. You know the people I mean.

If you think it's bad at school, know that it gets much worse in the adult world. Customers, clients, colleagues, bosses, lovers, and spouses are not going to let the spoiled person have his or her way all the time. Astonished by others' reaction to their demands, the spoiled person becomes depressed. Why is everyone so mean to her? No one has ever expected her to compromise before.

I know some teachers who have quit teaching because of parents who spoil their children—parents who demand that better grades or awards be given to their children to prevent their little darlings' feelings from being hurt.

This is harmful to their kids.

When a school official is badgered into giving you a music award that you don't deserve, you get two things: the award, which is meaningless, and the misimpression that you can always push your way into getting what you want.

Not true.

Learning now that you are not the best at everything you do is one of the most important lessons in life. You didn't earn the award, so does that mean you give up music? No. Do you decide to work harder for the next time or decide to teach rather than to play an instrument? Possibly. There are a million different ways to deal with the lesson of not winning an award. The wrong way, however, is to whine and plead and threaten others so that you get the award anyway.

Think about some of the other compromises you could be making now to enhance the quality of your life and the lives of others you care about. Here's a little exercise to help you decide what to work on next in this area of your life.

Fill in the blanks, if any, that apply to you:

1. I've compromised/will compromise with my brother/sister by

   _____

   _____

   _____

   _____

2. I've compromised/will compromise with my best friend/girlfriend/ boyfriend by

   _____

   _____

_____

_____

3. I've compromised/will compromise with my parents by

_____

_____

_____

_____

4. I've compromised/will compromise with _____ by

_____

_____

_____

_____

I hope you could fill in at least one of these blanks. If you did not, go back and THINK. (Thinking is good.)

Striking a fair compromise does not mean you've been defeated. A compromise is a victory for everyone!

It's a recognition that other people have rights, too. And it should work both ways. As someone very wise once said, "No man would listen to you talk if he didn't know it was his turn next." That's how life works. Everybody should have a say. Decisions should be the result of compromise between people who respect each other.

Even on my TV program, I do let guests have the last word unless, of course, they make a last-ditch attempt to mislead you.

And one more thing (there I go again): school and growing up are not like trying to earn money in a competitive world. In a competitive world you *have* to make compromises. If you pull the "my way or the highway" routine, you are going to do a lot of traveling.

And chances are you'll be broke.

So start practicing compromising now. It's what life in America is all about. If you believe that, your life will become much easier.

EYEWITNESS REPORT

Maybe, if we had an abundance of morality in this country, I could go to school without knowing how my friend's father ran off when he was born and left him with his grandparents, or how a third of my classmates' parents have been married at least twice or are single parents.

—*Thomas*

I can't please both parents. See, Mr. O'Reilly, they are divorced, and they ended up that way because they think totally differently. So, pleasing one parent inevitably leads to disappointing the other.

—*Philip in California*

My father has not paid child support, and I'm getting the blame. When I ask for something, I always get put down because of my dad's problems.

—*Julian in California*

Every day when I get home from school and my mom gets home from work, if she gets mad at work, she will slap me. I do not call this child abuse; I call it an everyday thing. I want to live with her because I do not want to live with my dad in Maryland. And I have to go before I get slapped for telling you this.

—*Anonymous*

My parents have been divorced since I was 1. Now, I'm a 12-year-old girl and live with my dad. I travel 50 miles every other Friday to visit my mom and 50 miles every other Sunday morning coming back to my dad's house. Sometimes I get stuck in the middle of their petty arguments, and I get to listen to my parents say bad things about each other . . . Divorced parents is really a sad thing, if you think about it!

—*Cassandra*

DEALING WITH
DIVORCE

W hen I was a kid, I rarely heard of divorce. Most of the parents I knew were religious and believed that marriage was sacred. At least, that's what they told us kids. Also, most of them didn't have enough money to support two separate households. Of course, I didn't understand that at the time.

Nor did I understand that there was probably a lot of anger, distrust, and cheating going on in some of those homes.

So which is better? Unhappy, toxic marriages that become a prison for both spouses? Or today's situation, where just about half of the marriages in America are likely to end in divorce?

I don't like either of those alternatives. Maybe that's just me. People ought to be very careful, not casual, about making the decision to marry. Parents ought to recognize that divorce can be very painful for their children. People who once loved each other, if they did, should try to work very hard at hearing each other and making compromises.

But this is not a book about adult issues. Someone else will have to come up with brilliant answers to this problem for them.

Meanwhile, you may be dealing with the fallout of divorce in your own home. If you are, you are going to have to be very strong. Here are some guideposts that may help:

1. **DEPRESSION.** Typically, even if you know that your parents' marriage is about to split apart, the actual divorce will probably make you miserable. It hits hard. And that's natural. Knowing that you will feel bad may not help you feel much better right away, but it's a start. There's nothing wrong with you because you feel pain. There's everything right with you.

2. **ANGER.** You may find yourself blaming one parent, or both of them. You have the upper hand here, if you really want to turn your parents' life into a living hell. But do you? Your parents are already suffering the emotional stress of their breakup. They don't want to lose you, too. I know that you may want to slam doors and dive into Xbox games or run off to a friend's house. Okay, let off steam if you have to. Then grow up. Think about the others in this situation, too. You're smart enough to know that these two people, even if they're yelling at each other, are in pain. Adult pain. If you can't keep your anger under control, get involved in some extracurricular activity that keeps you late at school or arrange some sleepovers at a friend's house—anything to put space between you and the situation until you can calm down.

3. **GUILT.** You are not the reason your parents decided to divorce. Again, you are not the reason your parents decided to divorce. There is nothing you could have done to cause or prevent it—not make better grades, not clean up your room, not get an afterschool job, not babysit your sister without complaining, not win the lottery and give them a gazillion dollars. Nothing.

Nada. Zilch. Divorce is between a man and a woman. That is the law. Even if there is another man or woman in the picture, the divorce itself occurs between those two people alone.

4. **GOING BACKWARD.** And if you didn't cause the breakup, it's logical (right?) that you can't do anything to bring your parents back together. That's not your job. Meddling only causes them more pain and sets you up for more disappointment.

5. **GETTING THE PICTURE.** You can't do this right away, but soon you should sit down and figure out what the divorce will likely mean to your life. Some of the practical questions you might want to ask are as follows: Will you be going to a new school because you'll move with one parent to another neighborhood or city? Will there be less money to spend on clothes and fun things because your parents will be supporting two households now instead of one? Will you have to help more often around the house? You may not like the changes that divorce brings about, but you are old enough to face them. You have to deal with them. Other changes may not be so obvious, so you should be on the lookout for them. Will your mother get depressed and stop taking care of herself? Will your father be embarrassed to talk with you openly now, since the marriage has failed? They will need you to help them. You must try to be there for them. In doing so, you will help smooth your own adjustment.

Yep, it's easy for me to say these things. My parents stayed married until my father died. They had disagreements. What am I talking about? They had fights. But things were different then, and it never occurred to my sister and me that they would divorce. That thought wasn't even on the radar. There may have been uncomfortable moments, but we never had to deal with your biggest problem: the loss of stability.

A major part of your life is broken. Knowing that half your friends are in the same boat does not make the journey less treacherous. You will want to cling now to everything in your life that can possibly provide you with stability: your closest friends, adults whom you trust and admire, familiar activities that are healthy for your mind and body, books that center your thinking.

But here's what you must avoid:

1. **DO NOT TURN TO ESCAPISM. DON'T ISOLATE YOURSELF. DON'T SHUT OUT THE WORLD.** Make more contacts with other people than you ever have before. Talk about the situation; don't keep it inside.

2. **DO NOT LET ONE PARENT TURN YOU AGAINST THE OTHER. IF HE OR SHE TRIES, SAY CLEARLY THAT YOU LOVE THEM BOTH AND DON'T WANT TO GET CAUGHT IN THE MIDDLE.** Explain that you have your own emotional problems and don't need theirs, too. If you refuse to take sides, only a very bad or disturbed parent will keep ragging you. You will have to take on the tough task of becoming "the grown-up" in this situation.

3. **DO NOT MAKE DRAMATIC CHANGES IN YOUR LIFE RIGHT AWAY.** Don't drop off the hockey squad. That's self-defeating. Don't pierce your ears and get tattooed or dress like a stranger. Although you know you need stability now more than ever, you may find yourself seeking just the opposite. But that's just a way of running from the pain of loss, a way of trying to wipe out the past.

You've lost the stability of marriage in your household. You should not let that loss drive you to lose the other things that are good in your life, too.

Have I said anything helpful? Maybe not. But we've been talking for a few pages, and that can't hurt, even if you think I'm a pinhead on this subject.

This is another of those times when I'd really like to hear from you. Tell me where I'm right or wrong. Tell me what you've learned that I ought to know about divorce today and its effect on kids. I sometimes talk about the subject on *The Factor* and I'm always willing to learn more about it if I think it can help someone.

Remember, you can always reach me via e-mail at O'Reilly@ FoxNews.com.

EYEWITNESS REPORT

I think it's wrong for adults to put you down or throw something on your shoulders just because they're having problems with something . . . It's not right for other people to think they rule over someone else just because they're older.

—*Keith in Mississippi*

I'm tired of being treated by adults as insignificant and a nuisance to society. People assume teenagers today are out to steal, disrupt, and destroy everything in sight . . . I think adults need to remember that they were once teenagers and treat us with the respect we deserve.

—*Sarah in California*

The biggest problem in my life is having to deal every single day with adults that don't understand us.

—*Stephanie*

My biggest problems involve adults like you that make decisions making this world a harder place for my generation to fix once we're in power. So I guess the biggest problem I face is that my opinion is silent when yours, Bill, is so widely accepted. No-spin zone? Think about us, for once.

—*Anonymous*

Personally, I think the biggest problem for young men/women is adults. The world we live in is currently very screwed up, and since adults are the ones running it, I can't help but think that the fault is theirs. Aren't people supposed to get SMARTER and MORE MATURE as they get older?

—*Elyse in Michigan*

OTHER ADULTS

I hope you're not the kind of pinhead kid who thinks that adults are living in a world that has nothing to do with yours. Sure, this book is about the special nature of the teen years. And sure, you're having experiences or thoughts that you might not want to share with most adults. But if you think that older people can't understand you, you're dead wrong. Although a lot of them seem dull, too busy, uninterested, and downright old, there are a few good reasons why you should look closely at the adults around you:

1. **SOME OF THEM, LIKE YOUR PARENTS AND TEACHERS, HAVE MADE IMPORTANT CHOICES IN THEIR LIVES BECAUSE OF YOU.** I'll tell you in a minute what I mean.

2. **MANY OF THEM KNOW THINGS THAT YOU WANT TO KNOW RIGHT NOW.** They may have money smarts, dating advice, or knowledge of a school subject you'd like to do better in. You'd be nuts not to ask them for help.

3. **SOME ADULTS—OFTEN FOUND IN YOUR OWN FAMILY OR IN YOUR OWN NEIGHBORHOOD—ARE LONELY, HAVE MONEY PROBLEMS, OR MAY EVEN BE DEPRESSED OR ILL.** And despite their wrinkles or fat, they're just like you. You can't be so busy or self-involved that you'll ignore their need to spend time with younger people. Visit with those people from time to time and you'll be the winner. Their life stories and wisdom will surprise you!

4. **OF COURSE, THERE ARE ALSO SOME ADULTS WHO ARE TOXIC. THE GROWN PERSON WHO WANTS TO BECOME YOUR FRIEND BY OFFERING YOU ALCOHOL OR DRUGS IS YOUR ENEMY.** And that's true even when, or especially when, that "adult" is the parent of one of your peers. An extreme example of such a toxic adult would be a sexual predator, but I'm warning you about something more subtle than that, as I will explain.

So . . . let's look at those groups of adults more closely.

Parents, teachers, and other adults who are doing good things for you: As I've already said, you are now mature enough to think about the feelings of others. You're smart enough to figure out what kind of effect they're having on you.

Look at your parents. How much of their day is devoted to you? Working to get money to buy your clothes or to buy tickets to the movies, cooking or cleaning the house or straightening your room, driving you to school, to sports practice, or to a party? Do you think that all of these activities are fun for them? (Hint: They are not.)

As for your teachers, they may very well enjoy their jobs, but what about the extra effort they make for you? Are they paid more for directing the school play, taking you on a field trip, or chaperoning a dance? They could just grade a paper, but what about the extra time they invest in writing you a personal note or offering you extra help?

When you were a child, you expected older people to take care of you. They should have. That's natural. Now things are changing. As you become a more independent young adult, you can see how hard certain grown-ups in your life are working for you. Try to look at things from their point of view. Learn from them . . . because you'll be in the same position someday.

Mentors: We can learn from books, we can learn from the classroom, but some of life's most important lessons are learned by working with an adult who has a special skill or knowledge we desire, too.

Sometimes you can be surprised by the things adults can help you discover. You think that an uncle is teaching you how to work on your car; then suddenly you realize he's also teaching you about how to do things for yourself. The time you spend with these adults is a time for growth. They've been where you are. They've made mistakes that they don't want you to make, too. I'm not talking about someone who lectures you. I'm talking about older people who are willing to work with you, listen to you, laugh with you, and respect what you say.

In today's busy, complex world, your parents may not be able to spend as much time with you as they'd like. But your aunt may have time to teach you how to do your hair so you'll look great at that party you're going to. Or Mr. White down the street may have time to look at the way you swing a bat and suggest a better approach.

Does this sound like an impossibly ideal world to you? I don't think so. Look around. The adults you know are probably a great untapped resource in your life.

Lonely, ill, or bored adults: No one likes a whiner, and it's true that some adults seem to feel sorry for themselves. But you'd be surprised, I think, by how quickly they can cheer up when a teen spends time with them.

I'm not suggesting that you start your own visiting nurse service. But when you offer to do an errand or help in the garden or bring over a book, you bring a little joy into an older person's life. Of course, if you think of visiting her as a job, nobody will benefit. But if you truly like the older person you're reaching out to, you will both end up as healthier human beings because of the time you spent together. We all need companionship. No one wants to be alone. If you think that adults are never lonely, you have a lot to learn. If you knew that a few minutes spent with an older person could ease his loneliness, why would you ever choose to spend those minutes alone with your Game Boy instead? Helping someone out, even an adult, makes you a better, stronger person.

Toxic, poisonous adults: There aren't many, but it takes only one to mess up your life. Sometimes the toxic adult is someone who looks like an adult on the outside but has never really grown up on the inside. She wants you and your friends to like her and her son, so she lets you all party in her house while she's at work. Is she a nice, understanding adult? No, she's a fool, and you should walk right out of her house.

Here's a rule to remember: Adults who don't act like adults are dangerous.

I don't mean that an adult can't have fun or relax around you. I mean that every adult in your presence has to act responsibly. Every adult is supposed to look out for you even when they don't make it too obvious because they know you want to be independent.

One of my favorite words for the teen years is "balance." As long as things are cool, you can enjoy your independence. But when things go bad, you need to be able to rely on adults because, kids, there are a lot of situations out there you cannot handle by yourself . . . and you should not have to try.

So if you know an adult who is not going to look out for you, if you know an adult who wants to be your peer, you would be smart to stay away from him because, as I hope I've made clear earlier, there are many, many other adults who can enrich your life by acting like the adults they are.

But if you trust the wrong adult, it could be disastrous. Be watchful. If your conscience or intuition kicks in, it's telling you to get away from that person . . . fast.

Pinheads and Smart Operators:

INSTANT MESSAGE Number 1

In a book of this length, I won't be able to cover everything in detail, so I've come up with a few brief O'Reilly i-messages for you.* They're scattered throughout the book. Some are about teenage pinheads; others are about kids who are smart operators.

CMIIW . . . **A Pinhead** is a kid who insults or argues with his parents or siblings in front of other people. There's no excuse for this behavior, not ever. It's not clever, even if it makes some jerk bystander laugh. Keep disagreements with family members where they belong, behind the closed doors of your house or apartment.

IMHO . . . **A Smart Operator** is a kid who always, always keeps her word, even, and especially, when circumstances change and keeping a promise becomes more

---

*Although this book is intended for you teens, I know that interested, caring adults may want to read it, too. In fact, you may want to share chapters with them specifically to help start a dialogue. Because adults don't instant-message with quite the same ease or frequency as you do, I've included a glossary of IM terms (page 187) for them.

difficult than she expected. If you promise to pay for something, then run out of money, the promise still holds. It's up to you to come up with the money, not an excuse.

A Pinhead is a kid who drives his parents and teachers nuts by delaying, complaining about, or refusing to do homework. SMHID. It's an hour or two of work a night, probably. Why add three hours of whining, harsh words, door-slamming, and all the rest? That's just not smart.

A Smart Operator is a kid who turns around and heads right out the door when there are no adults around at a kids' party. You know why. The adult doesn't have to be in the room snappin' to OutKast, but one of these specimens must be somewhere on the premises in case they are needed. Again, you know why. IRMC.

A Pinhead is a kid who thinks it's cool to drive fast or recklessly, hoping to impress or scare other kids. Black ice, guardrails, big trees, and semis were made for just this kind of pinhead.

A Smart Operator is a kid who doesn't blame anyone else for his own mistakes. The dog does not eat his homework. A friend does not make him late for curfew. The teacher does not fail him because she dislikes him. These things never happen to this kind of smart operator; he takes responsibility for his own actions. He's going to have a very good life.

A Pinhead is a kid who gropes or gives wedgies to other kids of the same or opposite sex. Wrestling is one thing; making physical advances is stupid, wrong, insulting, and possibly illegal. No one has the right to touch anyone else in a sexual way without permission. That includes the dancing called "freaking." Is it macho to grope some pretty girl? No. I've already told you what it is. GAL . . .

A Smart Operator is never afraid to try new things: exotic foods, music that is unfamiliar (country, classical, reggae . . . whatever), a foreign movie, a sport she's never played. If something appeals to millions of other people, whether it's ballet or cooked snails, there must be something to it, even if it looks odd at first. Never be afraid to learn. GFI.

A Pinhead drops out of school. "Failure to complete high school is almost equivalent to economic suicide," says Dr. Neeta P. Fogg, an economist who specializes in the problems young people face trying to find work. What she means is that the uneducated kid is likely to remain the unemployed kid, broke and out of it. Columnist Bob Herbert of the *New York Times* reports that roughly five and a half million people ages sixteen to twenty-four are out of school and unemployed in America. You do not want to join that club.

YOUR
Private Life

EYEWITNESS REPORT

Teens' biggest problem is money. Either we don't have enough or we have too much. You may say, Why too much? Because most teens do not know what to do with their money. I personally don't have enough to meet my desires.

—*Ashlie in Texas*

My dad lost his job last week. I don't [know] what I can do now; I am 10 years old. I wish I could magically get my dad a new job. Maybe, I could get a job myself. The thing that bothers me most is that my dad is a hard worker and one of the greatest dads out there.

—*Kevin in New York*

My biggest problem(s) is too much schoolwork and not having enough money to buy an electric guitar. Pretty lame, huh?

—*Chris in California*

You know how we teenagers wanna have our own money and spend it on whatever we want? Yeah, but ME!!!, I just wanta help my parents and have my own money at the same time . . . I don't care what others say, but I wanna work NOW!! I don't care what I'm gonna work at, but I just wanna have my own money, and help my parents.

—*Ericka in Florida*

YOUR MONEY

B y now you've probably observed that money is extremely attractive to the average American. We pursue it and spend it with vigor. But money is something that needs to be handled with great care.

I learned early that money talks. And I also learned that if you don't respect it, it walks out of your life . . . quickly.

When I was a kid, I didn't spend money foolishly for one very good reason: I didn't have any.

My father worked hard to support us, and my mother controlled the spending on food, clothing, and the other necessities associated with raising two children, my sister and me. Even back then, life was more expensive in New York than in most other parts of the country.

So my parents thought that Job One was saving for college expenses and retirement. That meant that we didn't get an allowance, an idea that struck my father as crazy. We didn't get paid for doing household chores, either. Those responsibilities came with living in the house and eating three square meals a day.

Just like you, though, the list of things I wanted stretched longer every day. But if I wanted something, I had to earn it somehow.

If I sound like I'm complaining, I'm not. Necessity can sometimes lead to a lot of fun, and that happened with me. When I was thirteen, I cut lawns, babysat, and shoveled snow. Later, my friends and I painted houses in the summer. Working together and keeping a sense of humor became a strong aspect of our friendships.

We also got in trouble sometimes . . .

My Story:

One summer five of us were painting houses in the neighborhood and making great money. But it was hot, dirty work. It was also hard work, because you had to be neat so the house would look really good when you were done.

One day we were all tired because we had gone to the movies the night before. We were painting the upper part of the house when all of a sudden one of the guys knocked his paint can over, splashing white paint all over a green bush that fronted the house. That bush was so white it looked like there had been a snowstorm in August. We all just stared. This was a disaster, because we should have covered that bush with a drop cloth before we started. But we hadn't been thinking.

Everyone looked at me because I was the crew chief. I yelled at the kid who did it: "Cohen, you dunce! Geez!" But yelling at Cohen was not going to solve the problem.

So here's what we did. We threw a drop cloth over the bush and went home after cleaning up. That night we sneaked back after everyone in the house was asleep. As quickly and quietly as possible, I chopped down the bush and we hauled it away.

We finished the paint job two days later. The owner of the house walked around inspecting our work and said, "The house looks nice, but there's something different about it."

Smiling, your humble crew chief replied, "Everybody says that after we finish . . . I guess because two coats of paint can really change the way a house looks."

The guy kept shaking his head, but to this day I don't think he knows that we removed the bush. He paid us, and I kept my mouth shut.

What I should have done was admit that we wrecked his bush and paid for it. But I wasn't up to being that honest. I should have been . . . because I still feel a little guilty about taking his money under false pretenses.

And you know that I'm going to say this: along the way, those of us who worked during our teen years all learned the value of money.

Sorry, but that's the truth. When you've worked a week to get enough money to buy the latest-style jacket, suddenly that jacket might not seem worth it. I started thinking that maybe the money earned during those forty hours of my life should really be put toward something else. I began to contemplate the relationship between hard work and the money it earns. I also began to realize that I did not want to live the rest of my life on low wages. These are two valuable lessons: what you do with them is up to you. I began to study harder. I did not, repeat NOT, want to paint houses for the rest of my life. It was too hard . . . much worse than studying.

Maybe you have all the money you want and all of this doesn't apply to you, but I doubt it. I've met some of the richest people in the world. I won't name names, but I've never met one who is satisfied with the millions or even tens of millions they have. There's always something else to own, something else to control. It's as if the need to have more is controlling them—*money* is controlling them.

For a smart, successful life you have to start learning right now how to keep money on a leash.

Here are some danger signs that will warn you when you are about to surrender to the money demons:

1. You buy something at the mall, bring it home . . . and wear it once or never. If you've ever done that, then you've spent your money like a fool.

2. You borrow money from a friend . . . and get upset when she asks you to pay it back, because you've spent it, so it's "gone."

3. Or you "lend" your friends and acquaintances money whenever they ask . . . but then tell them that you really don't need it back, hoping they'll like you.

4. You beg your parents to let you use their credit card. In my book—uh, this one—they ought to have more sense but maybe they just want to accommodate you too much. Get this straight: a credit card is not money; it is a contract to pay up to three times what an item is worth once you factor in the interest. Do the math. A credit card should be used only as a last resort, and then only for emergency items. You are stepping up and asking to be swindled every time you use credit. Unless, of course, you pay off the entire balance every month. And you probably don't. That would be un-American!

5. You don't try to understand where money comes from in your household, how it gets there, and where it goes. I knew what my father made, but I stupidly assumed that he could spend it all as he and my mother wished. Yes, apparently, I had never heard of taxes, fees, or property maintenance. Find out how much of your household's income is really "disposable" rather than "already spoken for," and you will have learned an important life lesson.

Tell the truth: are you possessed by any of these money demons? If not, you're lucky. But if you are, start exorcising them right now. They will make you their slave and make you unhappy if you don't.

Go to the business section of your local newspaper almost any day and you'll find out what happens to adults who are ruled by the money demons. Read about the millions of personal bankruptcies that occur each year. Not all are the result of bad money management, but many are. Each bankruptcy leaves one or several lives in disarray. Look at the rising amount of credit card debt.

Does all of this sound boring to you? It shouldn't. You're old enough to know better. Money is essential to living the good life in this country. Learning how to earn it and manage it is essential to your future happiness.

I hope you've heard of the great old comedian Groucho Marx. "Money frees you from doing things you dislike," he said. "Since I dislike doing nearly everything, money is handy."

I wouldn't go that far, but here are two good rules from O'Reilly:

Money enslaves you when you go into debt; money frees you when you can earn it doing something you enjoy.

Respect money. Don't waste it, borrow it, steal it, or hoard it. Earn it, use it to make your life more secure and, of course, use it to help others. If you do that, you'll never have to worry about the money demons.

EYEWITNESS REPORT

I did some smoking when I was 9, and I quit a while ago, but I have that in my system and I smell cigarettes when my dad smokes, so I get these urges. I don't smoke, but I am secondary smoking, and my dad keeps saying he'll quit, but he doesn't.

—*Seth in Ohio*

Nowadays, you have to have a boyfriend and be going all the way with him! Then on top of that, you have to do drugs, drink, and smoke!

—*Anonymous*

I just smoked because my cousin smoked and her friends smoked, and she was two years older than me. I felt like I had to . . . I smoked for a while, and then I stopped. I decided for myself.

—*Irina in New York*
[quoted in the New York Daily News]

SMOKING

I t will shorten your life.

It makes you smell like exhaust fumes.

It stinks up your clothes.

It costs a lot of money.

But you know all that already, and still some of you are going to keep on smoking cigarettes.

Sure, you've got a million reasons, and they're all stupid. Here's the truth: you've been hooked. You're addicted, and some of the most powerful adults in the world are determined to keep it that way. I'm talking about the tobacco companies and the politicians who use your parents' tax dollars to help keep tobacco farmers in business.

Did you ever think about that? No, you thought it was just a kid thing—that it shows you're independent, or cool. You might even think that it's your "right" to smoke like a burning oil field in Iraq.

No. You're wrong. Smoking is a scam. Getting you to take up the habit is an easy way for multimillion-dollar companies to rake in even more multiple millions. That's why they spend so much time, money, and sleaze on cigarette ads that can only appeal to fools . . . as if lighting up a weed will make you rich, popular, or good looking.

Excuse me?

As I said one night on *The Factor,* "Big business sees the ordinary American as a consumer, not a fellow citizen. They want your money even if it means your life. We're there to be had."

That's right: if you're smoking, you've been conned by some real evildoers. And if you don't get strong enough to quit now, you're going to have an unhealthy, shorter life.

My Story:

I have three quick smoking stories for you. When I was eleven years old, somebody gave me a cigarette and I puffed on it. I hated it. I inhaled once, and that was it. I couldn't figure out why anyone would want to smoke, even though my parents did. (When the health warnings came out later, they stopped.)

Anyway, I simply made the decision not to smoke. Then when I was twenty-nine, I was offered the chance to be the Marlboro Man. This was a very famous advertising icon in America, in case you're too young to know. An agency wanted to put my face on billboards smoking Marlboro cigarettes . . . and they offered me a lot of money to do it. But I turned it down. Thank God. (Perhaps you've seen one former Marlboro Man in an antismoking spot on TV. He filmed the public service announcement shortly before he died of cancer.)

The reason I didn't take the Marlboro job was that by that time I really disliked smoking. Why? Because I couldn't stand to kiss girls who smoked. One time I was out with a great-looking flight attendant who kept lighting up every few minutes. At the end of the evening she wanted to smooch. Believe me, it was like licking an ashtray. What a shame.

Recently a friend in his twenties who smoked for the past three years told me a story that backs up my point. A surgeon who was concerned about his smoking asked him to visit a university lab. In two separate jars were human lungs in alcohol. One set was pink and plump. The other was shriveled and almost black. One pair had come from a dead thirty-year-old lifetime smoker, the other from a sixty-seven-year-old nonsmoker.

You know which was which. My friend stopped smoking immediately.

Look at the ashtrays you leave in a room. They're choked with filth. Walk into a bathroom or a room set aside for habitual smokers. You feel gassed. Look at the ash stains and burn holes on your clothing. Yes, this is a very ugly habit.

And check out your teeth. Is yellow your favorite color?

What about the other people in your life? Everyone knows now that breathing secondhand smoke can be very dangerous to nonsmokers. You're taking their nonsmoking choice away by releasing your exhaust fumes anywhere near them.

You say your parents smoke? Then take a good long look at what they've done to themselves. Bad breath? Coughs in the middle of the night? Dry, papery skin? That's not just age, kid. Smoking adds five years to your looks and takes many more off your life. You did read what I wrote about the Marlboro Man in the ads dying of lung cancer, didn't you?

But you aren't listening.

You're hooked.

You've been scammed.

Kick it. Now. Or you're in for some major pain!

EYEWITNESS REPORT

Alcohol is everywhere in schools. 12-year-olds can easily get it. Alcohol is the root of the entire drug problem. The alcohol leads to pot. The pot leads to teenage sex. The sex to an entire string of problems that could have been easily avoided.

—Santo in Texas

A large majority of the people at my high school and neighboring high schools smoke marijuana and do other hard drugs such as cocaine and crystal meth. Even more teenagers abuse alcohol. All of these problems lead up to more drop-outs, teen pregnancies, and violence.

—Michael in Mississippi

My father has severe alcohol problems, which (I believe) leads to my parents poorly managing their money, causing fights between my mom and dad, and jeopardizing my ability to go to college. They make every day almost unbearable.

—Becki in Texas

ALCOHOL

I like many things about you kids. Most of you are warm-hearted, funny, active, sincere, filled with curiosity, helpful . . . all kinds of good things.

But here's one thing I really like about you all: if the teachers I know have it right and if the current research about your values is correct, you are a generation that is less likely to abuse alcohol in adult life than today's adults.

Drugs . . . that's another matter, but I'll address that in the next chapter.

Graduation nights, prom nights . . . also another matter. At certain schools, usually in wealthy neighborhoods and often abetted by stupid parents, scores of kids will drink to excess. Some of them have to be carted off to the emergency rooms, unconscious and suffering from alcoholic poisoning. You can die from that, by the way.

But a growing number of you, most of the time, seem turned off by drinking. Is that because you see adults around you who have become jerks or have ruined their lives by drinking too much? Have you seen, or experienced, physical or emotional abuse because of alcohol? Those are my guesses.

When I was your age, I learned a major lesson about drinking.

My Story:

Myles, a friend of mine from my high school hockey team, was left in charge of his house by his parents when they took a weeklong vacation to Florida. Since he was seventeen, they felt that he could handle the responsibility.

Wrong.

Myles invited nearly the entire junior class to a party at his house while they were gone. Many of these guys showed up with booze. I tried to help Myles keep things under control. But forget it. Guys got drunk, threw up, broke furniture, started fights, smashed windows, and pretty much destroyed his parents' very expensive home.

There was no reasoning with these guys once they were blasted. I knew them, but I no longer recognized them. Finally the cops came and threw everybody out. Myles was devastated. I don't think he ever got over it.

And my impressions that night have stayed with me, too. I vowed then that I was not going to drink alcohol. The scene just didn't appeal to me. Especially the getting-sick, losing-control part. I mean, nice guys turned into destructive animals. I didn't want that kind of experience, period.

To this day, I have never been drunk or stoned. I've tasted alcohol, but it leaves me dry. I don't need it. Given my highly public position, I've avoided many problems by not drinking.

For some reason, though, the sight of these drunks did not deter everyone in my gang. Maybe it was because they obeyed the rules so much of the time that drinking gave them an excuse to act out.

Maybe, because sex was officially a no-no, drunkenness was an excuse for having sex. Maybe some of them were depressed because they didn't believe they had any prospect of doing well in the world. Some of the people I knew who started drinking at age fourteen never stopped; they died much too early from alcohol-related accidents or alcohol-related diseases.

Well, that's my generation, not yours.

Of course, MADD (Mothers Against Drunk Driving) and other organizations have encouraged stricter laws against driving under the influence.

TV public service ads also remind us of how dangerous drinking can be.

And I think it's a brave and helpful act when a famous actor like Ben Affleck admits that he can't control his drinking and lets the world know about it.

Even the manic emphasis on body image these days is helpful in a way. The diet books stress that alcohol consumption leads to weight gain, and the exercise videos tell you how much physical activity is needed to counterbalance each ounce of alcohol you drink.

Most of you know all of these things.

But for the few who don't, here are some questions . . .

1. What percentage of kids in your high school drink and act stupid?

   _____

   _____

   _____

   _____

2. How much money does a steady drinker in your family or neighborhood spend on booze?

   _____

   _____

   _____

   _____

3. How many of your friends are unhappy or fearful because of the actions of a relative who drinks to excess?

_____

_____

_____

_____

4. How many times has someone you know done or said something hurtful because of drinking, something that he or she deeply regrets but can never take back?

_____

_____

_____

_____

In the television world I have seen many different kinds of drinkers. Some, like the NBC weatherman Willard Scott, found that their drinking threatened to get out of control when they had a major shock in their lives. After his wife died, Willard began drinking more heavily, but, as he has said publicly, he recognized the danger and, with the help of others, quit. One of the most famous TV executives in the world drinks so much in public that he has to be restrained from starting fistfights. Is he a captain of industry, or a jerk? I know people whose political or acting careers have been ruined by drinking, but I also know those who have had cocktails every day for decades and still maintain successful lives.

What does all of this mean? It means that, as in other things, you have to avoid being controlled by the outside force of alcohol. If you can't handle it, stop drinking. If you can't stop, get help.

I will keep saying this throughout this book, because it's the most important message I can impart: You have to learn to control your life with good sense. Otherwise, you will not find the happiness and success that are possible when you make smart choices.

EYEWITNESS REPORT

I am only 12 years old, and I am in middle school where people do drugs. I am sure I would say no if someone asked me, but if I was to keep getting pressured it would annoy me. And if I ended up doing drugs, my mom and dad would not have any trust in me. I just wish drugs would disappear. Wage a war on drugs!

—Brook in South Carolina

Me and my dad don't see or talk to each other any longer. I used to see him every other weekend. He was my hero. As I got older, I found out who he really was. He lied to me. He hurt my mom. He does drugs . . . It's hard to think that I don't have a father.

—Cecily

I was first offered drugs at the age of 12. And believe me, although I do not do drugs, it is not hard for a kid to get them, even in school.

—James in Pennsylvania

Suicidal tendencies and drug abusers . . . I go to a private school, so most kids here are rich. They use their money on drugs and horrid things like that. I get sad just looking at them.

—Kay in Mississippi

DRUGS

I f the experts have it right, more than half of you have tried drugs by middle school or high school, most likely marijuana. Because you've had "experience," you may think you know more than I do on the subject. As I've said many times before, I'm against drugs. In fact, I've never touched any kind of illegal drug in my life. But does that mean I don't know what I'm talking about? Let's see . . .

Maybe I can come up with reasons not to do drugs that will surprise you. I promise not to use the same old arguments that everyone else uses. In fact, I'm going to use the arguments I've heard from kids who are *in favor of smoking pot*, with an added question or comment for you to consider. Let's see if O'Reilly can make you rethink their positions.

Most kids who smoke marijuana claim it's a relatively safe drug. Playing the percentages, I don't believe that marijuana is guaranteed to lead to heroin, or worse. That can happen with certain types of personalities, but it's not true for everyone. So the argument that smoking pot can lead to worse addictions is valid only for some people, not for all.

Except in very rare cases, pot is also less likely than alcohol to cause traffic accidents. But does that mean it's safe? No. It means you guys think it's safER than most other drugs. But just understand that safER does not mean safe.

Most kids who smoke marijuana also say it's cool.

Really?

If you've tried it already, how did it make you feel, honestly? A little nauseated? Confused? Unable to make sense of what people were saying? Sure, you might have started off laughing, but how did the experience feel in the long run?

Most kids argue that there's no hangover.

Really?

You popped out of bed the next day, bright-eyed and eager to face the world? Breakfast happened in "real time"? You felt like you were actually "there" in school or with your friends?

A lot of kids also argue that brainiacs do it, too, not just the popular kids.

Really?

You're telling me that the best athletes, the most active leaders, and the most original students in your school are smoking marijuana? Most are not. Like many of you, they may have experimented—they may enjoy toking on Saturday nights at a party. But these people are rocking your teenage world because they are motivated, healthy, and hard-working kids the majority of the time. Like a brain surgeon who drinks a martini when he's not on call, the successful kids in your school may smoke pot on occasion, but they are not stoners.

Most kids who smoke marijuana say they can stop anytime.

Really?

Stop right now.

You know what I always say: Don't do things that prevent success.

Many of you can play around with marijuana for a few years, then get on with your lives.

But at what cost? How much do you miss in the classroom when you aren't entirely focused? Have you dropped out of school activities because you're too "tired"? Have you stopped seeing some of your best friends because they don't want to just sit at home, smoke, and listen to music? Have you considered how much you may be hurting your folks?

How much of the best years of your life are you missing out on?

I chose to address marijuana here because it is the drug you are most likely to try. I haven't mentioned the countless other drugs I know kids are experimenting with because that would entail a very long discussion—one that could fill a book of its own. But I do want to say, while I have your attention, that if you're using Ecstasy—especially the "designer brands" sold around schools today—you're really crazy. You have no idea what's in it, for starters. Beyond that, it is a drug that presents great danger to your mind and body, particularly to your central nervous system. It's a time bomb and you would be wise to stay away from it no matter what kind of physical pleasure it promises.

I've really tried to draw a fine line with my arguments here.

On the one hand, I know that you will not be terrorized or moralized into staying away from drugs, particularly one you think is relatively tame. About half of you will never try pot, they say. The other half is going to "experiment," knowing that most kids don't become raving maniacs or suicidal depressives because of social use of marijuana.

On the other hand, I really want to impress upon you the most practical argument against its use: doing drugs strikes me as such a waste. It's simply a practical argument. Relaxation is one thing. Hours of intentional, drug-induced downtime every week when you have so many other possibilities in your life . . . that to me is a terrible misuse of time, potential, opportunity, and youth.

Do me one favor.

Sit down, sober as a judge, and list the reasons you have been smoking.

Do they add up? Really?

List the reasons why you—not O'Reilly, not your parents, not your teachers, not your religious leaders—might want to stop smoking. These might be the things you miss because of your smoking: friends you don't see anymore, activities you cut from your life, or whatever.

If you don't agree that it's time to reconsider your drug use, you know where to find me.

And if you have never tried drugs, you've just learned what you're missing. Keep missing it.

Finally, here's why I have never done drugs . . .

My Story:

R emember the story I told you about my friend Myles and the boozefest at his house? Well, soon after that, drugs started to infiltrate my Long Island neighborhood. The year was 1968, and the Vietnam War was raging. Antiwar protestors used a lot of drugs in their antiestablishment lifestyles.

Pot came in first, followed by heroin. In New York City those drugs had been common, but never before in the suburbs where we lived. Right away, three of my friends got hooked on heroin. One died, two went to prison. Those two were never the same again. Their lives were ruined.

All of us in the neighborhood knew who the druggies were. For working-class kids, the temptation was strong. "Everybody" was trying pot. But I resisted. The booze thing helped me keep my promise to myself. I figured if I wasn't going to drink, why take drugs? I wanted to be different. I wanted to be strong. So I stayed away. And you know what? More than one of my friends who got screwed up on drugs has told me that I was extremely smart to forgo the experience. All of the druggies in my neighborhood told me they never thought they'd get hooked. But plenty of them did.

Drugs are a short-term high and a long-term disaster. Be strong. You don't need the experience. I don't know one single person who has ever said that he or she was proud of taking drugs. You have only one life, and you are unique. Don't let drugs or alcohol make you common.

EYEWITNESS REPORT

Just one time I want someone to hear what I'm saying about this: It is very stupid that people have to pressure someone into having sex. The pressured student will end up having sex so the other students will leave him/her alone. I just want to let you know this is my very firm belief.

— Tommi in California

Why not stop crying about abortion and how sex is dirty anyways? Why not educate us about it and teach us "safe sex"?

— Kyle in South Dakota

My largest problem is sex in the media and just in life in general. It is infused into areas where it's really not needed, and it pours over into kids' lives, and just wrecks them.

— Eric in Texas

As a male, a part of a sports team, and being well-known by students, I have seen the pressures of alcohol, drugs, and sex. Every weekend I am pressured to be engaged in one of these inappropriate activities, and the places I am pressured, parents are sometimes there, and sometimes not there.

— Peter in Maryland

The promotion of casual sex is absolutely appalling. I'm shocked every time I turn on my TV to sensual, suggestive, and promiscuous scenes.

— Whit

SEX

ome of your parents annoy me on this subject. They say, "Bill, you wouldn't believe kids and sex today. We didn't know half of what they know."

Sure, some of you know more of the basics than we did at your age, but I'm all for knowing the score, no matter what the game.

Thanks to some of the loonier films and magazines today, many of you know a lot about unusual sexual practices.

Thanks to certain priests in the Catholic Church and to other sources, you also know more about deviant behaviors.

Thanks to the worldwide pandemic of AIDS, you know more, I hope, about the need for safe sex, too.

And, according to many experts and studies, quite a few of you like to pretend that you're in the Clinton White House. I mean, you casually practice oral sex, even in your early teens.

I don't care how much you think you know.

Because knowing all of that stuff and more doesn't change a basic fact of life: healthy sex is a combination of sensible behavior and sincere affection. Listen to me: No matter how much you know about bodies, positions, practices, and preferences, you are nowhere near having the combination of maturity and insight that meaningful sex requires.

Don't get angry. No one your age, outside of literature, has had that combination. You're still growing in a million physical and emotional ways (which is why the teen years can be so difficult for everybody). As you've been told by everyone, teenage mood swings are unpredictable, dramatic, and often frustrating to others: giddy in the morning, depressed by second period, that kind of thing. All teenage emotions are volatile—it's an aspect of your physical and emotional development. No matter how often you have sex right now, no matter how ingeniously you position yourselves, you are years away from realizing your true emotions in this area.

Sure, your shoulders are getting broader, your breasts are becoming more prominent, but your emotions will continue to grow beyond that. They are going to become more profound, more experienced, more sensitive, more generous. For now, you have all the emotions you can handle, but believe me, there are more on the way.

I'm not going to bring in morality here. Some of you have religious beliefs that urge you to refrain from premarital sex. Some of you don't have such beliefs, or so you tell researchers. Many of you draw your values about sex from *The O.C., Sex and the City,* or worse. When I was in school, girls who had sex gained "a reputation." They were laughed at, scorned. Often those who had sex did so because they couldn't get a date unless they did.

Of course, that's changed. Today some of the most respected and accomplished girls will have sex, in some fashion. At a very upscale high school near my house, girls are teased mercilessly if they haven't had sex.

What's the smart thing to do in this situation? Well, I just hinted at one thing: don't have sex because the crowd bullies you. There is no more personal decision you'll have to make in life, so it's one you'll have to make for yourself. If you are not ready for sex, you're not "retarded." It might just mean you have better sense than others around you.

Here's another smart thing to consider: whatever you do, don't give the details to your friends. That is a betrayal of trust. I don't care if it was the best sex in your life. (At your age, that isn't going to mean much, is it?) It should remain an intimate, private matter. Once the gossip gets started, it can only turn around and hurt you. By the way, the person you have sex with IS likely to tell. Think about that before you do anything.

Here's one more smart thing you should think about: as you will learn for yourself after a couple of casual sexual experiences, it can be a real bore if you do not, as the old song says, "love the one you're with."

Now here's an interesting fact: in 2003 the National Campaign to Prevent Teen Pregnancy learned from polling one thousand teenagers ages twelve to nineteen that roughly nine out of ten teens said open, honest conversations with their parents would help them postpone sex until the right time.

But here's the problem: roughly one in four said they had never talked about sexual issues with their parents because they worried about their parents' reactions. It would really be smart for you to push past that barrier. If you're afraid that Mom and Dad will think you want to talk about sex because you're having sex already, point out politely and clearly that they've got it backward. Tell them you want to talk because you want to do the smart thing and because they know more than your friends do on the subject. Let them know you want their help. Of course, it will be hard to have this conversation, but I guarantee that your parents will appreciate the opportunity to have that talk.

Of course, it's got to be a two-way conversation. You should tell them what's on your mind, and then you must listen to what they have to say.

As for me, I'm not going to tell you to avoid sex, because in the end you will do what you want anyway.

I am going to tell you to look for love, though. For most of us, it's a lengthy search, but the challenge is fun, and the result, when you do find someone you respect, care about, and can laugh with, is the best. Some people think that's why we're here. Maybe so.

I am also going to tell you that while it's nice to be with a handsome guy or a beautiful girl, their beauty should not be just skin deep. You should like them for their personality, too.

Here's a big word for today: *dehumanization.* That's when you go out with someone only for their appearance—their big pecs or their long legs. When you are interested in someone only on the basis of physique, you're dehumanizing him or her, seeing that person only as an attractive object. If you are doing that, remember, good sex occurs between two human beings, *not* between two objects.

If you won't listen to me now, I hope that someday you're lucky enough to find out I'm right . . . because then you will have found an honest, rewarding relationship that includes sex.

Are you surprised by my thoughts on the subject? Did you think that O'Reilly would tell you sex is off-limits? As you know, things are more complicated than that. But I repeat my mantra: Sex is best when you combine sensible behavior with sincere affection.

That's the ideal, and it is smart to wait for it.

It is also smart to recognize that there is no area more potentially dishonest than the sexual arena. Girls, some guys will tell you anything to get that sex thing going. Then, after it's done, they will brutally drop you. Don't let that happen. Make your boyfriends prove themselves over time. And don't ever allow yourself to get drunk or stoned to have sex. That's how most girls get pregnant.

And guys, if you exploit a girl, it will come back to get you. That's called "karma." And don't allow yourself to be exploited by a troubled partner who wants to brag about her sex life to her friends, either. Believe me, you will come out a loser in that scenario.

Teenage sex is fraught with danger on many levels: sexually transmitted diseases, pregnancy, betrayal, and more. So learn to protect yourself emotionally *and* physically. And do I have to add that only a world-class jerk would neglect to use birth control when you're unmarried and having sex? Discipline yourself. Sex is not going away. It will be there when the time is right for you and your partner.

My Story:

I didn't have sex until I was twenty years old! Can you believe it? I was kind of a shy guy around girls, and I had absolutely no "moves."

At the time, I thought I was some kind of a loser. But then I started to see the consequences of other people's choices. Some of my more aggressive friends got girls pregnant. Some married those girls. Most of those marriages were disasters, and the children suffered. More than one of the guys I grew up with ruined his life, and the lives of others, because he had irresponsible sex.

That still happens today even though abortion is more common. And abortion has its consequences, too—many girls who have abortions suffer terrible guilt their whole lives. The bottom line is that this sex thing is big-time serious.

Looking back, I was darn lucky I had no moves. I had to wait for sex, and I'm glad.

EYEWITNESS REPORT

I think our youth has gotten lazy and they don't manage their time well. Instead of doing their homework, they sit and watch TV and let their homework pile up to the point where it does become a problem.

—*Brittney in Colorado*

TV has to have a bunch of bad words and naked people on all the time, like that is entertaining? Robin Williams is entertaining! I'm only 14 years old and feeling like they are messing up my future. How can I think about having kids after I go to college? If I have them, how can I protect them from all the sex and bad stuff on TV?

—*Leslie in Missouri*

The Lord Jesus wants me to be merciful, kind, humble, long-suffering, forgiving, and meek. One of my biggest problems is being influenced by too much secular television. Television such as MTV.

—*Brian in California*

The biggest problem kids I know have nowadays is that my rents [parents], along with all my friends' families, keep their TVs tuned to Fox News Channel 24/7. Regular TV programs are boring to them now. This has been going on for 26 months. What's weird is that, if a TV's on some other channel besides Fox, I can't get to sleep. Is this normal or what?

—*Logan in Indiana*

TV

Chances are, your first exposure to sex or violence was on TV. So here's some solid advice: take TV in the right doses, or you'll be in trouble.

I make my living on the tube because I want to talk about people who cheat and people who get cheated. I want to talk about ideas. I want people who watch my program to think, even if they disagree with me.

But most TV is not designed to make anyone think.

It's designed to give you dumb ideas so that you will spend your money on stupid products and never learn to think for yourself.

So, should you turn the TV off for good? Take an ax to it? Hurl it off the fire escape?

No. Like so many things that you and I will talk about, TV is only good for you if you control it. It's a powerful tool. Use it. Don't let it use you.

Nothing can give you a quicker, more accurate picture of what's going on in the world than TV . . . IF you can trust the broadcaster to tell the truth without twisting it.

The tube will also put you right in the middle of some of the most exciting sports events of all time . . . and that's great, provided you don't let watching TV coverage become a substitute for getting out there and playing on the field (diamond, arena, courts, pool, etc.) for yourself.

It's true that television programming is also filled with eye candy and fantasy, but a healthy person knows that it is important, sometimes, to relax the body and the mind . . . AS LONG AS you don't begin believing that you have to have a girlfriend who looks like Buffy and cars like the ones they drive on *24*. These fantasies don't have anything at all to do with the real world.

Commercials can also be entertaining . . . IF you don't buy into all their claims. "Buy me, then you will be sexy/rich/happy/slender/buff/smart" . . . You know the list of promises they make.

Of course, the claims are not always that obvious. They're hidden. "Drink this beer because it tastes good" actually means "Drink this beer because then you will have lots of good-looking friends and lots of fun." When all of the guys and gals in the ad are actors who are chosen because they look like the people researchers think you want to be, you can be sure advertisers are using hidden messages to persuade you to buy their goods.

It's not just ads directed to you that are laden with such powerful suggestions, of course. The companies that want your parents to buy a "luxury car" (I'd say "overpriced gas guzzler") use actors who look like wealthy, powerful people. The truth, of course, is that the actors are probably waiting tables or tending bar much of the year to support themselves and could never afford to buy that car, but that's another story.

The word for the messages that TV ads use is *subliminal*. It means they're speaking to your unconscious. If the ad said straight out, "Use hemorrhoid medication and you will be happy all day because you'll own a beach house," you'd laugh. But look at the images in the ad. That's what the subliminal message really is.

It all comes down to this: whether you're watching TV commercials or programs, you have to use your head. It's only when you don't think for yourself that watching TV can become dangerous to your mental and emotional health.

I mean that, and here are some warning signs:

1. **IF YOU GET DEPRESSED ABOUT YOUR WEIGHT OR YOUR LOOKS OR YOUR SOCIAL LIFE BECAUSE THE KIDS ON A PARTICULAR TV SERIES HAVE IT SO MUCH BETTER THAN YOU,** get a grip. These shows are written to amuse you, not to reflect real life.

2. **IF YOU HAVE TO RUSH OFF TO THE MALL THE INSTANT YOU SEE SOMETHING ADVERTISED,** you've been tricked. Did you need this item before you saw it on TV? No? Then you don't need it now.

3. **IF YOU FIND THAT YOU ARE GETTING YOUR VALUES ABOUT FAMILY LIFE OR SCHOOL LIFE FROM A TV SHOW,** watch out. Sure, there are many programs that are written around positive life lessons. Just make certain that you can tell which ones are and which ones aren't.

4. **IF YOU ARE TALKING MORE TO YOUR FRIENDS ABOUT WHAT HAPPENED ON A TV SHOW THAN WHAT IS HAPPENING IN YOUR REAL LIFE,** you've got your priorities wrong. And you're definitely watching too much TV.

5. **IF YOU ARE FIGHTING WITH YOUR FAMILY ABOUT WHICH SHOWS TO WATCH,** step back and look at the reasons. Is TV worth all of the conflict it's causing in your home?

6. **WHY WOULD YOU WATCH A RERUN?** Maybe there's a good reason to see something you've already

seen, but I can't think of one. Find something else to do. Read.

7. **IF YOU'RE TIRED IN THE MORNING,** if you're falling behind in school, if you're slowing down on the athletic field, if you're short-tempered . . . there could be many reasons, but one possibility is that you are watching TOO MUCH TV! **IT'S NOT HEALTHY TO BE THAT PASSIVE FOR SEVERAL HOURS A NIGHT.** Your body and mind are telling you to cut back.

Ever notice that the more channels you get, the less there is to watch? I don't know why, but it's true.

On the other hand, there are some great television programs available today (in addition to *The Factor*), if you choose them rather than letting them choose you. History, science, great music and drama, up-to-the-minute news, lively discussions—all of these things can be found on TV and can make you smarter, wiser, and even happier . . . if you make the remote your mentor, not your jailer.

And one more thing (I'll stop this soon, I promise): time is valuable. Don't waste it. Taking a walk or reading anything short of porno is better for you than some dumb sitcom. Even keeping a diary of your life will pay off as you grow up.

But watching TV excessively rarely pays off. It can actually prevent you from growing up!

EYEWITNESS REPORT

I think teenagers' biggest problems are trying to stay in style by dressing the right way, listening to the right music, and acting the right way.

—Keely in California

It seems that nearly 95% of the kids at my school don't care about anything but what they hear rappers talk about.

—Edgar in Illinois

I feel constant pressure from peers who are "popular" on what should be worn, how we should act, and what our hobbies should be. I feel like it is all a result of music, especially hip-hop.

—Roger in California

MUSIC
MADNESS

A sixteen-year-old guy e-mailed this comment to me the other day: "I agree with you on almost everything, but you are wrong when you speak about Eminem."

Here's only part of what he heard me say on TV about the famous rapper: "Eminem is a nasty piece of work whose recordings have sold in the tens of millions . . . The guy is exploiting angry kids who listen to him."

Okay, you're not surprised by my reaction. Every generation flocks to the music-makers who seem to speak only to them, not to their parents. For me, it was Elvis and the Beatles, now revered worldwide as musical geniuses. But back in the 1960s they were considered a very bad influence by some of the parents in my neighborhood. The parents of my day grooved to Frank Sinatra and Bing Crosby. We kids thought these two guys were old and had no rhythm or life in their music.

We were wrong, but so were the dissenting parents. We wanted our own music with our own messages. If parents were outraged, so much the better. They thought Elvis was a thug. They thought the Beatles were British wimps with sissy hairdos. They thought our music didn't have good words or melodies. Of course, we thought our parents didn't have a clue. And we were right.

Here's the point about all this: some new music we can't imagine yet will be out there next year or next month, but my advice will still hold true.

And that is . . . listen up for yourself. You can like music your parents don't get, but you don't have to like it just because you think every other teen does. Don't get swept away by the hype. Make up your own mind about what music you like. Eminem sells millions. So what? Let him sell billions. Does that mean you have to go along with the crowd? Allen Iverson is an amazing basketball player. You can admire him for that without buying his rap CDs. They dis women and gays and use gutter language. Do you think it's cool to play an album with dirty, sexually explicit lyrics when you know your parents won't like it? How infantile is that? About as infantile as Eminem's latest CD.

So how do you decide when music is bad for you, possibly even dangerous? Actually, I think you already know the answer to that.

If a song incites you to feel hatred toward someone else, white or black or gay or foreign, it's ugly and bad.

If a song shouts that women are put on earth just for the sexual pleasure of men, or otherwise puts women down, it's dangerous.

If a song espouses taking money, acting out violent feelings, killing yourself, or drowning in drugs as a means to be "free," it's not music, it's madness. And just because a song doesn't have lyrics that hurt or threaten you personally doesn't make it acceptable. Any song that glorifies destructive behavior IS destructive. Period.

Still not convinced to choose for yourself? Then look behind the scenes of the music business. Just like the hustlers selling tobacco (see the "Smoking" chapter), record company execs see you only as part of a lucrative business proposition. Their business, like most others, is designed to make people part with their money. And your generation happens to have a lot of disposable cash. (That's right. Advertisers targeting your money think you are the richest generation to date—they call you the six-pocket generation because they think that you not only have money of your own, but that you can get money from your parents and your grandparents, too!) How much do you spend on CDs every month? How many of last month's do you still listen to? Do the math. You're a target for a reason.

Along with CDs, the corporations want you to buy a thousand other related items: new CD players with unnecessary bells and whistles, clothing that is supposed to make you look like a rock star or a "gangsta," books and magazines and posters. There's nothing wrong with being a fan, but becoming a groupie may mean that you need to get some perspective.

It's fun to listen to music that's new; it's fun to share it. It's fun to argue about whether "emo" or "ska" or "screamo" is worth listening to before they vanish from the scene. But if you're papering your wall with CDs, you're falling into a trap—one set up for you by the music execs who just want your money. Remember, you've got the power. Why do you suppose Mariah Carey was fired from the record label she recorded for? Because of *you*. Not enough young people were buying her latest CD. You drive the market. But do you know who I think is the smartest in this whole situation? Those guys and gals who are performing and taking your money, because they're actually doing something. They're exercising and developing their talents, not just sitting around.

My Story:

I've always liked music. My tastes are all over the place. I still listen to Elvis, the Beatles, the Beach Boys, and other stuff I grew up with, but I listen to lots of new music, too.

I don't like rap and I think gangsta rap, in particular, is a total fraud. If you do what these guys and gals say they do, tell your parents to get bail money ready. Did you know that gangsta rap is the most popular music in prison today?

But . . . I know I'm out of touch with the rap world. So I'm not going to tell you what to listen to. I will suggest, though, that you sample all kinds of music, including the "oldies." Music should be fun. Sometimes it should be carefree and should make you want to dance. Other times it should help you relax and make the time pass on long drives.

But no matter what you favor now, one thing is for sure: your musical tastes will change as you get older. Some of the songs I liked when I was a teenager are, well, incredibly bad!

So what defines good music? The answer is in the ear of the beholder. That's why there are so many different kinds of music. But the message of the music is something else.

No matter what your friends think, you don't have to listen to music that makes you uneasy or offends you. Music should bring out your deepest feelings, the whole range, from joy to yearning. It should not make you angry or violent or disrespectful.

You've got your own pair of ears, your own smarts, and your own right to turn off the bad sounds.

DUMB FAN SIGHTING

A teenage driver wearing a headset with the music turned up to the max, veering through traffic: Mr. Cool? Sorry. Not even close. This is deadly dangerous to the driver and to the other people around him. Traffic accidents don't wait to happen between songs. If you're in the car with this type of person, get him to stop this stupid behavior . . . or get out.

Finally (aren't you happy "one more thing" is history?), the world of rap and rock is just like the world of TV—it's one you want to control. Don't let it control you. Becoming obsessed with any form of entertainment will stunt your personal growth and prevent you from becoming a well-rounded person. If you're attached to your MP3 player for hours at a time, watch out.

Life passes quickly, and a mind is a terrible thing to waste. Rock on, but do it as recreation, not as an escape from the real world you have to live in.

EYEWITNESS REPORT

I have too much stress. I'm only 13 and I should be using my youth. Being the top class of school, they always look at us. "Oh, you should do this, you should do that." What they should do is let us have fun while learning. All we have done this year is work, work, work . . . no fun, no trips. I'm personally sick of it.

—Jennifer in New York

Kids pick on me, I hate writing assignments, and sometimes school lasts too long. We don't get to have any fun in the 5th grade.

—Jason in California

Keeping things positive is the biggest problem of my life.

—Kylie in New Mexico

I think the biggest problem is not having enough time to be a kid.

—Jenna in Colorado

Stress from my family, stress from school, and stress from friends . . . I thought that 8th grade was supposed to be fun, but at the moment it's like a big knot is tied up inside of my stomach and I'm about to explode with all the pressure.

—Jeanette in Florida

FUN,
FIRST OF ALL

I mean it . . .

If you don't enjoy life, all of the money, fame, and possessions you pile up will mean nothing. You'll be bored . . . and boring.

At the same time, you have to balance fun with the rest of your life. It's not healthy fun if . . .

1. IT **INTERFERES** WITH YOUR FAMILY AND SCHOOL RESPONSIBILITIES.
2. IT **COSTS** MORE MONEY THAN YOU AND YOUR FAMILY CAN REALLY AFFORD.
3. IT'S TRULY **DANGEROUS** OR INVOLVES SUBSTANCE ABUSE.
4. IT **HURTS** SOMEONE ELSE'S FEELINGS OR INVOLVES YOU IN USING ANOTHER PERSON.
5. IT LEAVES YOU TOO **EXHAUSTED**.
6. IT'S AGAINST THE LAW.

Sorry to start with negatives, but now that we've got them out of the way, let's look at some of the positives. Write down a list of all the things you find the most fun, even stupid things.

If you really enjoy sticking a french fry in your ear in order to get a disgusted reaction from a girl, write that down, too. No one but you will see this list, so have fun with it.

If you enjoy doing something that a friend thinks is "nerdy" or "gay," know that your secret's safe with me. Write down whatever you like doing, no matter how silly or embarrassing you think it is.

Even if you have fun doing something that breaks one of my six O'Reilly rules above, write that down, too. For instance, if you're a bully and you think you enjoy pantsing a kid who's younger or weaker, include that. This little list will ultimately serve as a tool for you to look at yourself and consider what your tastes in fun really say about you. So be honest.

Your finished list will be like a profile—you know, the kind the FBI puts out when they're looking for a serial killer. (Okay, I'm just having some fun with you here.)

But really, this list presents a snapshot of who you are inside. Now let's look at it together.

Although I can't see your list, I can suggest some questions you might want to ask yourself about it.

Do you have the most fun doing things by yourself or with others? Or do you enjoy a little bit of both?

Do you have the most fun reading and watching? Or do you enjoy writing and performing more?

Was teasing other people on your list? If so, do you really enjoy it, or is something else going on?

Does anything on your list surprise you?

Did any activity that you routinely engage in with your friends NOT appear on your list?

In other words, are you doing things that you really don't want to do? I mean, do you go to a certain party or dance in a certain way because "everyone else" thinks it's fun, but you really don't? Are you pretending to have fun just because you feel peer pressure? Take some time and think about these questions. Revise your list several times if you have to.

You may even change your list as you look it over again. That's okay.

But hear me loud and clear: Do not cross off something that you really like doing because you think someone else will think it's nerdy. If you haven't learned this lesson yet, learn it now. It is dumb to discontinue an activity that gives you healthy fun just because some pinhead knocks it. I don't care whether it's engaging in a science project or a rollerblading contest, playing the violin or practicing for a marathon, writing poetry or joining the debate club. Anything that is fun, in a healthy way, is a response to the true inner you. If you are not doing the things you find fun, you risk starving your inner soul. (Don't ask me just what that is; you know what I mean!)

You should, however, reconsider any items on your list that make you uneasy. If you were afraid to write them down, that says it all. If you think they say something bad about you, then it's time to discontinue them.

Over the years, some of the ways you have fun will change, naturally. Just think what used to be fun when you were three or four years younger. You should be open to these changes. It's how we make room for new experiences.

But we need to pause here for a warning . . .

It's dumb to let yourself overdose on fun. That's what I meant by rules 1, 2, and 5. Too much fun is like too much ice cream; you can get sick of it. You do not want to become one of those kids who is always trying to get other people to ignore their homework or cut class to "have fun" instead. That's being a jerk. The cool person finds fun even in those things that are required of him, like practice or homework.

I know some very successful guys in the TV business who were class clowns during their school days, but let me tell you something, they quickly learned when to joke around and when not to. That's how they became as good as they are at what they do today: they learned how not to go too far. A couple of jokes may be fine, depending on your teacher, but then you have to settle down to work. The best class clowns are never fools.

Same thing with trying to party every night. Parties are the dessert of life, not the main course.

People who have fun in their lives are always ready for a laugh, but know when it's appropriate and when it's not. Some people even believe that laughing can reduce stress and make you live longer. You've probably heard the old saying, "Laughter is the best medicine." Well, I think that's true. It certainly can help you and your friends through some bad times. I'm not talking about cruel laughter, as you know. I don't believe in making fun of someone else.

I'm talking about healthy laughter—the kind that helps us sit back, look at a bad situation, and put it in perspective. And few things in life are smarter than learning to laugh at yourself. That's a skill that keeps you sane. It keeps you cool. It helps your friendships, because if you can laugh at your own flaws you will have more patience with the flaws of other people.

As important as humor may be, however, there are times when your sense of humor may not be the same as a friend's.

This is tricky stuff. Just as sharing the same sense of humor with someone else can help you form a special bond with that person, not having the same sense of humor can cause rifts. Sometimes we don't like people because their sense of humor strikes us as creepy, nerdy, cruel, or just plain stupid.

This important distinction takes us back to what I said about having fun at the beginning of this chapter. What you define as fun provides strong clues about the true nature of your personality. I'm not saying that you will never feel friendship for someone who has a different sense of humor. But humor does say a lot about someone's character. There are some very decent people who do not have much of a sense of humor. You can deal with that on a day-to-day basis, but your lifelong friends will probably be people who laugh at the same things you do. Humor is an important part of how you deal with life.

I know I've been serious here about having fun . . . but I've had fun doing it! I really enjoy sharing what I know about life to help you enjoy yours more.

Here's some other stuff I enjoy, too: snorkeling, watching pro sports, bodysurfing, playing touch football, watching movies that teach me something or are funny, kayaking, hiking in the autumn when the foliage changes colors, playing chess, ice skating, and reading books about something I didn't know. Am I boring? You make the call.

Pinheads and Smart Operators:

INSTANT MESSAGE Number 2

A Smart Operator is a kid who musters up the courage to ask for help when she is having trouble in class, in sports, or anywhere else. The problem won't go away by itself. If you already knew everything, you wouldn't be in a learning situation to begin with, right? So take advantage of the resources around you. If you're too timid to speak up in class, write your teacher a note or get help on the weekends from a good friend. Don't let things slide.

A Pinhead is a kid who spreads stories about other people. It makes no difference whether or not they're true, although most times they're not. Once a tale goes around, it's out there forever. Decades from now, when you meet a friend from school, you will both remember the stories you heard about other people. Lives get ruined this way. Let the tale stop with you. Make it very clear that you're not interested in hearing it or sharing it. DEGT.

A Smart Operator understands that manners make life better for everyone. "Good manners are different from knowing which fork to pick up or how to order in a fancy restaurant," notes *The Teen Quiz Book* by Annalee Levine, Jana Johnson, and Arlene Hamilton Stewart. "They're more about courtesy and kindness." Knowing when to call an older woman ma'am and when not to are the kinds of social rules one can easily learn. But real manners go deeper than that. Real manners entail behaving in a way that makes things pleasant for others around you.

A Pinhead is a kid who brags about how much money she has or how much money she's spent on something. You have to hope someone will tell her how stupid she sounds. Did she get these vast sums of money because she earned them? IDTS. So she's got nothing to boast about.

A Smart Operator is a kid who gets a decent night's sleep so that everyone else doesn't have to suffer with him the next day. When you don't get enough rest, you're cranky at home. You're not going to pay attention or do well in class. You won't be able to exercise or play sports to your full capacity. This is a common problem for teenagers, thanks to the changes under way in your body and to the challenges of your social life. But you're just going to have to face it squarely. If you're not able to go to sleep before midnight or if you wake up for hours in the middle of the night, you should probably talk to the school nurse or your physician. They may be able to suggest some remedies.

A Pinhead is a kid who shoplifts. And especially a kid who says that "it's fun!" Shoplifting is theft. Theft is a crime.

95

In some countries, thieves get their hands cut off. That's a bit much for a tube of lip gloss, but it's worth remembering. When you steal, you cause prices to be raised for everyone else. Still, that's not the point. Theft is wrong (refer to my chapter on "Cheating"). And it's definitely not proof of how clever you are. Just the opposite.

A Smart Operator remembers the birthdays of friends and family members. (Write them down.) You don't have to buy expensive presents to make someone happy. Any mention or kindness will make their day. You're saying, "I'm glad you came into the world on this day, and I'm glad that I'm lucky enough to know you." By the way, you don't have to wait for birthdays. Get up early some morning and surprise your parents by doing some chore that's usually theirs. Showing appreciation to others is always the right thing to do. IYNWIM.

A Pinhead gambles. There's a reason why state-sponsored lotteries are called "the stupid tax." The odds are stacked against you in every kind of gambling there is. It's the losers who pay. And the winners? Rare. Very, very rare. I've never understood people who claim that "it's fun" to gamble away their money. I work too hard at earning mine; it's no fun for me to see it disappear. And gambling, like drugs and alcohol, can grab you by the throat, get you addicted, and ruin your life.

YOUR
School Life

EYEWITNESS REPORT

I'm 15, and the biggest problem in my life is trying to fit into a place where there are very high expectations on how you are supposed to act, look, and dress. Fitting is hard.

—*Sharlene in Washington*

A girl in school makes fun of my clothes that aren't from American Eagle and Abercrombie and Fitch. Our family is on a pretty tight budget, and we don't have exactly a Willow Bend house or anything like that. I get clothes from Kohl's and Target, which probably aren't the cutest clothes ever.

—*Jackie in Texas*

You should see some of the stares I get when I wear *The Factor* jacket to school!

—*Corey in California*

THE DRESSING GAME

If you don't look like Britney Spears, should you dress like her?

Probably not. (Don't worry about that. Some of her body has been acquired through surgery.)

Listen, you don't have to tell me that teenagers' ideas about clothing change every month. The TV advertising execs, the mall stores, the movie and music honchos all see to that. (Hey, did you really think you came up with those "fashion statements" all by yourself?)

What you wear, who you copy fashionwise, or how quickly styles change may worry or confuse your parents, but I know that teens have their own ways of looking at clothes.

You'll laugh, but when I was in junior high school, we thought girls looked sexy in pink mohair sweaters, long tight skirts, and little white ankle socks. (Okay, you can stop laughing now.)

Our parents didn't get it, either. But here's the most important thing: They also never understood which girls were dressing sexily as a come-on and which ones were just slaves to fashion. In other words, they didn't understand the language of our clothing choices.

That means your parents and I probably don't understand the language of your clothing choices either. And since I can't comment on what I don't know or understand, I'll quote others who do.

A high school teacher recently told me this: "Kids don't feel the same way about nakedness as we did. It's not about being sexy."

Hmmm.

I don't get that. But I do know that you know how to "read" what spaghetti straps, lowriders, and navel rings mean and don't mean. You know which girls and boys are dressing to advertise their availability and which ones aren't.

I once taught in a school in Florida . . . Perhaps we should pause as you try to imagine me as your teacher. Have you recovered yet? Anyway, off campus some of the girls dressed so skimpily they would have been arrested and flogged in some parts of the world. I wasn't shocked by this kind of clothing. It just looked ridiculous. To me, they were awkward kids trying to look sophisticated. But it didn't work.

Although I don't understand the language of your clothing, I do know what can happen if you choose clothing that sends the wrong message to other kids. School is a place for education, but also for fun, and looking good is part of the fun. However, kids who dress provocatively can be making some very stupid choices. I want you to be smarter than that.

I don't want to bring you down, but I can tell you that some of the girls who dressed to impress guys in my teen years had some very sad experiences. Many of the sexy dressers attracted the kind of boys you know they attract. That sometimes meant getting into one abusive relationship after another. And you can guess what happens in a relationship based on appearances rather than respect—when the guy gets tired of your look.

You got it. Many of these girls got dumped! Luckily, some of them caught on in time and learned to play the clothing game with smarts. They realized it was dangerous and stupid to attract trashy guys who would only exploit them.

And what about boys?

The situation is not quite the same for them.

No matter how provocative their getups, they're not going to be taken advantage of in the same manner as girls. It's the way of the world. So what's sexy dressing for a boy? Depends on your town, school, section of the country, even your social class. But let me share with you something a young woman told me long ago. "Nothing is sexier on a man than a crisp, clean white shirt . . . with jeans, with shorts, with anything." Try it. It works.

Sex is a major part of a healthy life, as we've already talked about. But not knowing how to use sexual appeal, and how to keep it in perspective, can be dangerous.

If this is just what your parents tell you, they're right. You don't have to dress like an old man or a nun (unless that's the latest fashion fad). But you should dress like yourself, whatever that is. Only then will your clothes send the right message to other kids.

Someday you'll have to learn the language of adult clothing if you want to succeed in the world, so it's a good idea to practice now. Sure, there are computer geniuses and authors who get respect even if they dress like geeks and bums, but they're the exceptions to the rule. Most of us adults dress in clothes that show our intent.

When you see me on TV, I'm wearing a tie, dress shirt, and business suit. Do I dress like that all the time? Of course not. But that clothing makes a statement. According to today's adult tastes, I'm serious about my job and respect my guests and my viewers. Wearing a powdered wig made that statement centuries ago, but tastes change. So you see, even adults have to learn to adapt to changing fashions, too.

There's an old saying that "clothes make the man." Of course, this is not really true. But your clothing choices are a basic part of how you present yourself to the world. They speak for you, so it's smart to choose carefully what they say.

And even if you do look like Britney Spears, you should think twice before copying her style of clothes. She has bodyguards.

As you know, I'm interested in your thoughts. My e-mail, which I mentioned earlier, and office mailing address are printed in the back of this guide. And as I've also said earlier, I really do want to hear what you think, so don't be shy. Write to me.

Here's a specific question you might want to answer for me: What do you think of the following dress code, which was announced at John Jay High School in Cross River, New York, for the 2001–2002 school year?

Regarding dress, grooming and appearance including hair-style/color, jewelry, makeup and nails a student shall:

1. Be safe, appropriate and not disrupt or interfere with the educational process.
2. Not wear extremely brief garments such as tube tops, mesh tops, halter tops, spaghetti straps, plunging necklines (front or back), micro-minis, short shorts, bare midriffs and see-through garments.
3. Ensure that underwear is completely covered with outer clothing.
4. Not include items that are vulgar, obscene or libelous or denigrate others on account of race, color, religion, creed, national origin, gender, sexual orientation or disability.
5. Not promote and/or endorse the use of alcohol, tobacco or illegal drugs and/or encourage other illegal or violent activities.
6. Not include jewelry that can be dangerous, such as spiked bracelets or neck collars.

What are your thoughts?

And remember this: In a few short years you are very likely to encounter a dress code at your job. My TV network has one for young job applicants. One look at a tattoo, nose ring, tight jeans, or an exposed midriff, and you're out of there! We run an international news operation, not a dance club.

Is that fair? You bet. The guy who signs the check gets to make the rules. He wants people working for him who actually reflect the image of the company.

Dressing appropriately can help further your career and can even help you succeed big-time in life—and that's not a bad thing at all.

EYEWITNESS REPORT

We are 15-year-old twins in the 9th grade. The biggest problem we face every day are other kids that procrastinate, don't do their work, and CHEAT by trying to copy our work. All they want is a free "A" without earning it.

—*Angela and Amanda in Washington*

CHEATING

Cheating.

I hate it.

Many kids don't think twice about it. They assume that it's okay. In fact, according to research by the Josephson Institute of Ethics, nearly 70 percent of teenagers in the United States admit to having cheated.

Cheating is, of course, a form of lying. The same researchers found that nearly 90 percent of you readily admit to flat-out lying.

If I have an uphill battle here, that's fine with me. Because I'm going to try to convince you that cheating, like all other forms of lying, hurts you first of all, and the whole world in which we live, too.

Does that sound like an overstatement? Follow along . . .

When you cheat, you get something you don't deserve. At first that sounds okay: something for nothing! And what difference can it make? You get the good grade, you pass the course, you go on to the next course.

Except . . . you don't really know the subject as well as your grade suggests, and over the years you will fall further and further behind. You are in effect dumbing yourself down.

That's because you are developing the bad habit of disguising how little you actually know. When you get out into the real world, that kind of deception will hurt you. You're developing a bad habit that can lead to being fired, or worse.

My Story:

A secretary at a TV station where I worked was as charming, helpful, and seemingly efficient as could be. But then odd things began happening. Packages mailed from our office didn't show up at their destinations. We complained hotly to the post office, but even more went missing.

Then one night a cleaning woman happened across a pile of boxes and other large mail items in a closet . . . The secretary had never mailed them. Why? Because she did not know how to operate the office postage meter and was afraid to ask, since her application indicated that she did. Of course, she was fired.

You can't read the newspaper or watch TV news for a week without hearing about someone getting caught cheating in business or politics, and do you know why? Because cheating is addictive!

My first reaction was, how did that secretary possibly think she could lie and get away with it? But my guess is, she had done it so often in the past that it had become an unbreakable habit. Will she go on to do it again? If she had done it once before and gotten away with it, the odds are, yes.

Well, you say, not all cheaters get caught. You may know an adult who cheats a little bit on his taxes. You may know of a teen who cheats her employer out of a few dollars at the cash register. You probably know a kid who writes answers on the inside of his arm or leg before taking a test.

And every one of them, in your experience, gets away with it . . .

But do you respect them? Do you laugh along with them? Will you trust them to tell you the truth or come through for you when it's really important? Not unless you're really stupid. The person who cheats the government, the school, or his employer is not going to make an exception for you, or for anyone else. Cheating is habit-forming. It's an addiction of the weak. Pay attention now: The person who cheats will cheat you. It will happen.

And their cheating poisons us all.

That's what I meant earlier when I mentioned hurting the whole world in which we live.

We all know how it works. Here's how a high school principal in Connecticut explained the game in an article that appeared in the *New York Times*: "The students used the word 'contagious.' If they knew the kid next to them was doing it, and winding up with a higher grade-point average, it was difficult not to participate . . . But the students told me they'd had enough of it. They want it to stop. They need adults to take it seriously."

This adult does.

Trust is what makes us neighbors. Trust makes us all partners in this great country. When politicians get caught taking money on the side, or when executives get caught robbing the company or stockholders, or when athletes get caught using banned substances in competition, our society gets just a little more tarnished each time.

You may be a good example. I mean, it's likely that you are saying to yourself, "What difference does it make if I cheat? Everyone else is doing it. The rich and famous do it. That's how they got rich and famous."

That's called "cynicism," class. It's the refuge of someone who's given up. And it's very lazy thinking.

Because the truth is—and I know this from dealing with hundreds of successful men and women—that in the long run 99 percent of people get what they earn honestly.

Can you believe I said that? I mean, if you've seen *The O'Reilly Factor,* you've probably seen me talking about some liar in politics or crook in business.

But they are news because they're the exception. That, after all, is the definition of news. I suppose I could begin every program by saying, "Today, tens of millions of ordinary Americans did not cheat the taxpayers or steal someone's pension fund or overcharge a hospital for medicine." But that wouldn't be news.

Which is a darned good thing.

I want you to learn to be proud, if you're not already, of getting good grades and awards honestly.

I want you to recognize that having a conscience is a gift, not an obstacle, for living a successful life.

And one more thing . . . once you get caught cheating, you are branded. When I taught history in high school, I caught some students cheating on tests. Those kids lost my trust and my respect. Do you want to be branded a cheater?

I didn't think so. It is a painful brand. I know . . . because I was caught cheating once.

My Story:

I was a sophomore at Chaminade High School on Long Island, New York. I was taking Latin. For me, that was not fun. I worked hard, but I still didn't get a lot of it.

Once when I was taking a big test, I choked. I didn't know the meaning of a word, so I stupidly glanced at the paper of the guy sitting next to me. The teacher saw me, and I caught hell.

That was it. I never cheated again. I'd rather fail than be branded a cheater. And the good news is that I've succeeded in life, without ever cheating again.

Not ever. And that's huge.

EYEWITNESS REPORT

My mom, who just so happens to be a 5th grade teacher, says that when she has a student who picks up a book after they have finished their work, she praises them. What do you have to say about that, Mr. O'Reilly?

—*Kristen in Texas*

The biggest problem in my life is knowing what life is, who I am, and how to figure it out.

—*Anonymous*

I love learning, and I can't understand why everyone else doesn't.

—*Daniel in California*

Mr. O'Reilly, I am 15. My biggest problem right now is the fact that I cannot find time to go out and buy *Who's Looking Out for You?*

—*RJ in New York*

READING

I know something about your classmates . . .

Last night, one of them traveled back in time two hundred years to England and watched a pirate kidnap a young teenager and take him on a great adventure.

Another flew in a spaceship to a strange planet where there were three green suns in the daytime sky and where giant plants curled their strong tendrils around human beings and then ate them like cheese sticks.

Still another ran away from home and hitchhiked to San Francisco to get away from a drunken father . . .

Of course, I'm talking about their reading excursions. Reading can take you into and out of a million different places. A good book can scare you or make you laugh, teach you about distant lands and times, or make you cry in sympathy for another. Or better still, a good book can help you understand who you are more clearly. When you read a novel or short story, you don't need actors, a cameraman, or a director . . . your imagination supplies all of that, cued by the writer's words. Your experience of the book will never be exactly the same as that of anyone else in the world. Reading is creative play for your mind.

Of course, you know what I mean. You're reading a book right now!

The question is, what is the best way to make reading a regular part of your life?

First, let's agree that there are different kinds of reading, and that each requires a different kind of approach:

1. You read some books in school (and someday you'll read books for your job) mostly to get facts. To make that kind of reading work for you, it's smart to take notes. You don't have to write down every fact. Here's a memory shortcut that works for me:

   If page 47 of a book I'm reading describes the causes of the Vietnam War, I don't write down all of the causes. Instead I write, "P. 47, VN War causes." This helps organize my mind as I read. It also provides a quick road map to particular sections of the book for when I want to return to them later.

2. As you grow older and get more practice, you will be reading for ideas, not just facts.

   In this type of reading you are looking for the overriding point the author is trying to make. Facts are usually provided by the writer to help support this overriding idea. You can take notes when you do this kind of reading, too.

3. Then there's the kind of reading you choose just for yourself because you want to learn something on your own. The focus of the book might be on a hobby like cooking, chess, or computer graphics. You might read a self-help book to assist with a personal problem or to help answer serious life questions. When you engage in this type of reading, no one's testing you. You decide for yourself what is important to remember. You might skip the

section on cooking pasta because you want to cook risotto instead. You might decide that the self-help writer who provides personal advice is a jerk. This is recreational reading that you control.

4. Last but not least, there are the exciting, entertaining, and sometimes disturbing books—fiction or nonfiction—that can enlarge your life. Through these books, the world is yours! For pure escapism, you might develop a lifelong habit of reading science fiction, mystery, or romance novels. They're fun, and they keep the brain cells working. Sometimes you will want to try novels that have won prizes or have gotten good reviews. You won't like all of these important writers—no one does—but you will develop favorites among them. Great writing, like great music or great art, can inspire the best in you. As you grow older, you will better appreciate how a great book has something to say about the questions and challenges of your own life. And you'll never stop learning from nonfiction. What's going on in the country? What's going on in the world? What are the latest medical findings on exercise and dieting? How did someone you admire become so rich and famous? You'll find all these answers and more in your local bookstore.

Here are some facts I read recently that I don't like: according to the U.S. Census Bureau, the adults around you are likely to spend seventeen times as many hours watching the tube as they do reading books. And a Gallup poll taken in 1999 found that six out of ten adults read only ten or fewer books a year. (If they're reading what's on the bestseller lists, as opposed to the classics, that's not very challenging reading at all.)

You probably know someone who likes to check out the medicine cabinets in other people's bathrooms. I've never understood that particular form of nosiness, but when I'm in someone else's house I always check out their bookshelves. Sorry, but I can't help it. If you don't want me to do it in your house, be sure not to invite me over. Most times, I'm shocked. Some of the brightest people I know have either no books at all or nothing but mindless junk on their shelves.

Now, I'm not saying you should read just to impress other people, even me. I'm arguing that reading is as good for the health of the mind and soul as exercise is for the health of the body. Forget that it's good for you . . . it's fun, too!

Consider how lucky you are. The human race has existed for tens of thousands of years, but the common people (that's you and me, kid) have only been able to buy books and learn to read for roughly the last three hundred years. Billions of people around the globe, and I'm not exaggerating, are still unable to read today. Even if you disagree with every chapter in my book, what a great gift it is that you can read and react to it—without anyone stopping you! Tyrants have often kept people in slavery by denying them that gift.

When I used to cover stories in the field I often went into poor neighborhoods to report on crime and violence. But I also got to film stories about people doing good in those areas. I have seen grown people burst into tears because, late in life, someone finally took the time to teach them to read. When you've watched a sixty-five-year-old man cry because he can read a simple story to his grandkids for the first time ever, you will never forget how reading can bring joy to a life.

If you're still not convinced to make reading a part of your daily life, then here's the crusher: if you read on a regular basis, you'll be smarter than most of the people on this planet. And being smart is good. It leads to financial success and, most importantly, to a life full of adventure!

EYEWITNESS REPORT

Parents at odds, impossible siblings, getting by in school, it is all part of life. None of it gets to me. But I am faced with a problem that gets to me. It lies with myself. A daily lack of confidence in myself keeps me from escaping my safe little niche and taking some real risks. A terrible thing happens when you live a risk-free life, Bill . . . Nothing.

—Patrick in Florida

I am a 12-year-old boy in the 7th grade. I really have two big problems. The first is choosing the right friends that will help me stay on the right path. The second is my low self-esteem. I just scored a 33 of a possible 72 points on a self-esteem test.

—Jeff

Peer pressure, unreasonable parents and teachers, ridiculous media and all other outside forces are not the worst things I deal with. It's my own dark tendencies—my self-doubt, anxiety, inability to concentrate, etc. . . . I assume this is the price of becoming an adult and only a passing phase, but I'm probably wrong.

—Mike in Florida

I have a problem of trying to please others before myself.

—Zach in California

My worst problem is I'm depressed a lot of the time. Nothing helps. Well, that's it.

—Christopher in Georgia

I am 14 years old and one of the biggest problems in my life is a friend of mine. He has a lot of control over my emotions, being he makes me happy and sad.

—Caitlin in Florida

SELF-ESTEEM

The concept of developing self-esteem in children is one of the most abused on the planet.

Let me put it this way: it's a good idea that has been dragged through the mud by jerks—some of whom may be parents or teachers you know.

Here's what I think self-esteem should mean:

1. **YOU LOOK IN THE MIRROR AND FIGURE OUT FOR YOURSELF WHAT IS GOOD ABOUT YOU.** You decide what your strengths are (yes, you have some; we all do).

2. **WHILE YOU'RE LOOKING, YOU'RE HONEST ABOUT YOUR WEAKNESSES** (yes, you have some; we all do). Can you do something about them? Are they worth worrying about when compared with your strengths?

3. **YOU DO NOT EVER EXPECT ANYONE ELSE TO GIVE YOU SELF-ESTEEM!** (Does the word "self" ring a bell?)

Healthy self-esteem can help you accomplish your goals, but fake self-esteem can ruin your life. Before I talk about the good kind, let's look at the bad kind.

It started something like this: back in the 1960s, long before you were born, educators got the idea that every kid should be told that he or she is a special human being. Fine. That's the truth. You are unique. I'm unique.

But then this basically sane idea got screwed up. Certain people decided that each of us, for the sake of our self-esteem, should be protected from competition. In other words, they decided that kids should be protected from the real world. (Real educators should be teaching you about that very world, for your own good.)

Here's what I mean: I can't sing. I could prove that if you were within hearing distance, but you would suffer greatly, so just take my word for it.

Suppose, however, against all reason, I had decided in high school that I wanted to sing in the chorus. In my day, the music teacher would politely say no, as he well should, and that would be that. Enter the self-esteem police, who have greatly influenced the world in which we live today. According to them, my feelings would be hurt by this decision. I would feel rejected. My self-esteem would be damaged. So, in order to make me feel greater "self-esteem," the music teacher would be forced to accept me, and he, the rest of the chorus, and any unlucky audience we might entertain would be forced to endure my horrible yelps. But forget the music; I would have supposedly maintained my self-esteem by being allowed to participate in the chorus.

This is dangerous nonsense.

I have seen, as you probably have, this mad idea taken to weird extremes. A kid doesn't make the football team, so his father picks a fistfight with the coach, defending his son's self-esteem. A girl doesn't make the grades she wants in her favorite class, so her mother makes the teacher's life a living hell. (These types of parents are a major reason why good teachers quit teaching, as I've mentioned.)

Here are two things to remember whenever you see that kind of behavior:

1. **YOUR PARENTS WON'T BE THERE TO PROTECT YOU WHEN YOU DON'T GET A PROMOTION OR PAY RAISE AT WORK.** Preparing for the realities of the world outside high school now will help you to cope with them better in the future.

2. **FALSE SELF-ESTEEM IS NOT REALLY SELF-ESTEEM;** it's an emotional Band-Aid applied by someone else, and it will come off in the shower.

Let's go back to the real thing, the original notion of self-esteem. When you look honestly at yourself, you will be able to capitalize on your strengths and deal with your weaknesses. I couldn't sing, but I was smart and strong enough on the field to become quarterback of the football team.

So far, so good. I looked honestly at one weakness and played up one strength.

But I didn't go far enough, and I want you to go much further than I did. For example, I was too lazy, weak, or insecure to work on a third group of my characteristics: weaknesses that had the potential to be strengths if only I had been smart enough to work at them.

Here's what I mean. Maybe because I went to an all-boys school, I was terrible at meeting girls my age. My cheap clothes and gangly looks didn't help, but that's no excuse. I could have tried harder, asked for advice, or just persisted until I learned how to present myself to the opposite sex.

Also, because no one had encouraged me, I didn't realize that I had talent as a writer and speaker. I remember wanting to do more in these fields, but I didn't have confidence or what we now call (you guessed it) self-esteem.

And that's no one else's fault but my own. Since I wanted to write, I should have worked harder on my writing skills right then, instead of waiting until college. Revving up the necessary self-esteem was my responsibility, and I blew it.

To sum up, healthy self-esteem is good for you, if you develop it on your own by honestly looking at your strengths and weaknesses. The fake self-esteem doled out by some parents and teachers today is poison.

By the way, just for the record, my strong self-esteem, which is pretty obvious throughout this book, has nothing to do with the number of books I've sold or the number of viewers my television program attracts every night.

No, it comes directly from the inner O'Reilly. Finally, I've learned to believe in myself. I'm pleased with the weaknesses I've developed into strengths over time and the strengths I have developed even further, and I'm not ashamed of the things I can't do well. I simply enjoy those talents in others. It's a good feeling . . . and it's based on common sense.

EYEWITNESS REPORT

I am 12 years old, and I play football, basketball, and soccer. The biggest problem I face is juggling homework and sports.

—*Jeb in Virginia*

My biggest problem in my life is that our school has to cut sports because we have lost much of our funding from the state government, which has caused many of our students to leave our school, which is also what I may be forced to do.

—*Adam in Ohio*

As a student athlete, I always have a busy schedule, and it can be hard to find time to keep up my grades in a heavy course load while attending 2½ hours of basketball practice every day, not to mention maintaining healthy relationships with family and friends.

—*Allie in Ohio*

SPORTS

No one ever had to encourage me to play sports. From the time I could walk, I was throwing and catching things with my ruffian friends. Forget hand–eye coordination at age four or five. I just felt good running and jumping and climbing and playing like a maniac.

So it was natural for me to take up team sports like baseball and football as soon as I could hold a bat or throw a spiral. I was still playing quarterback in college. Today, when I see certain plays on TV, I catch myself imagining that I could do better. I know I can't, but the love of competing with others, of playing together with your teammates, of achieving something in a contest . . . well, that never leaves you.

My Story:

I know that I would never have succeeded in my career if it hadn't been for my sports obsession as a kid, because I learned so much, but there's a twist to my story.

When I was sixteen years old, I played in the Connie Mack baseball league on Long Island. I loved it. Then, suddenly, we had a new coach who did not like me at all (I know that's hard to believe). Anyway, he cut me from the team! And I was a good pitcher. To this day, I remember how angry I was at that injustice; I fumed for days.

My mother felt so sorry for me that she called up a team in another town and arranged a tryout for her angry son. But she didn't tell me about it until an hour before I had to show up. She knew I wouldn't be thrilled that my mom had to intervene.

Yet, it was one of the few times in my childhood that I grasped the big picture and appreciated what my mother had done for me. At the tryout I struck out six guys in a row. Not only did I make the team, but I became the ace pitcher. And this team had a far better playing field, with lights and dugouts, than my local team had. I played ball the entire summer and had a great time.

I also learned a huge lesson: life is not fair. But when you get screwed, you should use your anger to become even better at whatever it is you are doing. I vowed I would show that coach who cut me that he was an idiot. And I did. In other words, I used my anger in a positive way . . . and you can, too.

It doesn't matter whether you're on a team, in the band, on a debating club, or acting in a play. Performing and competing always make you stronger. Find something you like to do and get good at it. Show everybody, including yourself, what you're made of.

Now, I am perfectly aware that you might find sports boring.

Okay, that doesn't make you a bad person. But let me state the case for a second look. At this time of your life, your body is probably awkward. You might have so-called "growing pains," because your limbs may be maturing more quickly than the rest of your body. You might have trouble sleeping, or you may even sleep too much. Because of bad eating habits or lack of exercise, you might be getting flabby. For the same reasons, believe it or not, you might be feeling depressed.

Rise up, I say, and do something physical!

If you don't feel energetic enough, that's probably because you aren't playing something regularly. Does that seem like a contradiction? It isn't. When you play sports frequently, you get more energy. You feel better. There are good scientific reasons why, but we don't need to go into them, because you can see what I mean by looking around you.

Do the best athletes in your school slouch down the halls? They do not. They walk with a spring in their steps. (Sure, they're showing off sometimes, but they have the energy to put on the show.)

Exercise takes the flab off, gets the blood racing, and makes the lungs work harder.

But we don't play sports just for the effects on the body. That makes it sound like medicine. And if you go too far in that direction, you might be tempted to use steroids, which is not only dangerous but also a sick form of cheating.

Instead, think about the lifelong effects of learning to play together, or to compete fairly.

Once I was working in a TV studio where everyone was out to get everyone else. There were knives in the back, made-up malicious gossip, and dirty tricks to keep others off the air.

About that time, second baseman Chuck Knoblauch of the New York Yankees was having trouble hitting. But one afternoon, he led off the game with a base hit. Behind him came great hitters, all of them capable of slamming home runs out of the ballpark and getting the glory. But home run hitters are also likely to strike out when they're going for the big one. So each of these guys decided to act like teammates instead of egomaniacs. They all wanted to help Knoblauch reach home. The second batter hit a single. Then the third batter hit a single. Knoblauch was able to score and get his confidence back because his teammates thought of him rather than of puffing up their own records with another home run. And we're talking multimillion-dollar competitors being that generous here.

The shabby behavior at the TV studio was exactly the opposite of the kind of teamwork exhibited in that ball game. Of course, you don't have to play sports to learn to deal with other people fairly, but you can't play sports without learning that life lesson.

Here are some O'Reilly reasons for playing sports:

1. **EVEN THE SHYEST PERSON MAKES GOOD FRIENDS** when playing on a team or competing on the courts.

2. You don't know how good you can be at some activity until you **TRY AGAIN AND AGAIN TO BETTER YOURSELF.**

3. **YOU DON'T KNOW HOW GOOD YOUR BODY CAN FEEL UNTIL YOU'VE WORKED UP A SWEAT** and happily exhausted yourself.

4. **FEW THINGS IN LIFE ARE MORE EXCITING** than the up-and-down, back-and-forth scoring in a tightly contested game.

5. **YOU WILL GAIN CONFIDENCE IN EVERYTHING** you do.

6. **YOU WILL FIND OUT THINGS ABOUT YOURSELF THAT NO ONE COULD TELL YOU,** and when you know yourself, you will know how to make a success out of your personal and professional lives.

Let me repeat what I said earlier: I can understand why some people will pursue avenues of activity other than sports. There are many ways of learning how to work with other people.

But since a certain amount of physical exercise is necessary to good health, why not make getting that exercise an enjoyable experience through games and contests with other people?

For the rest of your life, sports skills will help you meet new folks in all kinds of social situations. You may pursue golf or bowling instead of touch football as you get older, but the effects will be the same. Sports activity provides an instant avenue of communication with strangers.

The Romans, as you may know, had an expression for the perfect life: *Mens sana in corpore sano.* That means "A sound mind in a sound body."

You don't need more than that.

Sports can take you in that direction even if you are not gifted athletically. Remember, you should play for fun and for fitness. Play for the fresh air and for the friendship. Smile, laugh, blow off steam. Swim, rollerblade, ski, run, surf, wrestle, golf . . . whatever you like.

Just do it. You'll thank me someday because sports can protect you against some bad habits—habits that you see on display every day.

EYEWITNESS REPORT

My teacher was extremely liberal and attempted to incorporate his personal views with the facts pertaining to the subject. I finally learned that to make a good grade in his class I would have to slant my writing and fake my views to coincide with his. Miraculously, after making this change, I saw an improvement in my grades. As a student, I should be able to take a class without having to worry about changing my opinions simply to obtain a grade. Education should be as unbiased as possible in order to be fair to the students.

—*Julia in Texas*

My math teacher doesn't teach, she gives examples. Her voice is so boring that you have two choices, sleeping or drawing.

—*Kelley in Washington*

My teacher drives everyone in the class crazy. She treats us 7th graders like we were 6 years old. Also about a month ago, my dad was waiting outside, and she told him she thinks I'm depressed and may need to "see" someone. I am a happy kid, but she, for some reason, thinks that because I don't put on a fake smile at every moment of the day I have problems.

—*Anonymous*

Five days a week I have to suffer through my physics class with the worst teacher in the world! I never thought one class could drive you completely insane. Most 16-year-old girls should be struggling with boy problems and their parents, but not me. I don't have time because I'm too busy trying to figure out why F=MA.

—*Brooke in Colorado*

TEACHERS

Every teacher you have is kind, smart, hardworking, and trustworthy.

Sure, and I'm Brad Pitt.

As a growing teen, you should be getting better at finding the balance between what's reality and what's myth.

Not all advice books will tell you the truth on this score, but I will. Some people in authority are more admirable than others. Most do their best. A few couldn't care less. This is just as true in the adult world as in yours.

You shouldn't be surprised that this rule holds true for teachers, too. Most of them, in my experience, work hard in difficult circumstances to teach you what they can—even when you resist. A few are so gifted that they will change the lives of kids in their classes for the better. Their lucky students will remember these teachers with gratitude for the rest of their lives. They don't make huge salaries, but they make a difference. I don't have to tell you, though, that there are a few teachers who aren't making the grade.

Here's a flash: you're not going to change that situation. But you do have an opportunity to handle it in a mature way. Not that I always did . . .

My Story:

Up until I was about fourteen, I was the class clown. Sometimes I was funny, but mostly I was just dumb. The truth is that all teachers can be dull at times, so I felt I had to liven things up. And I did.

One of my teachers, Aimee Martin, had to be eighty years old and was completely out of touch in the classroom. Of course, she thought I was a fool. And she was right—I made her life miserable.

I'm not going to tell you exactly what I did (because I don't want to encourage boorish behavior), but it involved sabotaging her lesson plans. I thought it was hilarious at the time, but again, I was a moron on more than a few occasions. The bottom line was that my dopey friends and I had a few laughs at Mrs. Martin's expense, but in the end she found out about it and my father was alerted. Not a good thing. Mrs. Martin had the last laugh. I was punished many different ways, including losing TV privileges for a month.

So what good did my dumb behavior do?

Making a bad teacher's life miserable achieves nothing. It's a waste of time. Your time.

Here are my guidelines:

1. **BE GRATEFUL FOR GOOD TEACHERS.** Listen and ask questions. Seek their advice. You are smart enough to know the difference between sucking up to the teacher and taking advan-

tage of her knowledge and skills. If your friends don't, that's their problem.

2. **IF CLASS IS DULL OR UNHELPFUL, LOOK FIRST AT YOURSELF.** Is it "boring" because you didn't do the homework, so you don't know what's going on? Is it unhelpful because you aren't fully prepared to take this particular course? Do you feel uneasy because there are a lot of strangers in the class? Are most of the kids older than you? Or are you the eldest in the class? Did you get enough sleep the night before?

3. **IN SOME CASES, YOU CAN DISCUSS YOUR PROBLEM WITH THE BAD TEACHER.** Teachers can be shy or awkward, too, and may not necessarily approach you about the problem first. Some will be grateful that you took the time to explain why a class is not working well for you. That is, if you don't just whine, "This is so uncool!" You need to approach the conversation with an open mind.

4. **BUT OTHER TIMES THERE ISN'T MUCH YOU CAN DO.**
   You can try getting transferred to another class, but that might be out of your control. Or you can do something you'll have to do many more times in your life when someone in authority is not very capable or concerned about doing well: you'll just have to shut up and get through it. The alternatives—acting out, causing conflict, making jokes—will only work against you and quite possibly lead to lifelong bad habits.

5. **BEWARE OF THE TEACHER WHO IS POISON.** Here are my candidates for that dubious distinction:
   Any teacher who wants to be your friend in an inappropriate way. You know what I mean. Don't be flattered and taken advantage of by an adult who does not understand the boundaries be-

tween teacher and student. Watch out. Yes, a wise teacher can give you good advice outside of class, when you ask for it. But teachers are adults, never peers, and they shouldn't act like peers.

Any teacher who insults you by expecting you to do badly or to fail. If you could learn the subject by yourself, you wouldn't need a teacher. If you are trying to learn, she should be trying to teach. For every doctor or lawyer or actor who says, "I did it even though my teacher said I didn't have the smarts to do it," there must be hundreds of people who just gave up. A teacher who has no confidence in her students' ability to learn has no confidence in her own ability to teach.

Any teacher who raises your grade or gives you an undeserved award because your parents complain. When that happens, both the parents and the teacher are wrong.

Any teacher who wastes your time.

I've been on both sides of the desk, as I mentioned earlier, and so I feel the pain of kids *and* teachers, too!

For two years, because I didn't know I could make a living in TV, I taught high school in Florida. Now, this is not a good reason to do something as important as teaching, but I worked very hard to be an effective teacher. I knew the subjects. I had strong feelings about my need to be responsible, as you already know. I wanted my students to learn, to tell the truth, to use their heads, to have a good time, to be fair to each other and to me, and to grow.

Other teachers were much better than I was, because they were naturally gifted, or they were very experienced, or they worked even harder than I did.

A few teachers were no good at all. They were marking time until retirement. They didn't like students. They had given up after years of frustration with the bureaucracy, among other things. One shuffled into school with obvious hangovers. Some showed films to their classes as often as possible, because they were too lazy to prepare a lesson. Others just didn't have smarts.

This all sounds familiar to you, I'm sure, but let's look at a positive story.

My Story:

I became a high school teacher after graduating from Marist College. That was God's way of challenging me because I had given so many teachers a hard time throughout my childhood. But I rose to the occasion and really enjoyed teaching English and History. I was tough on students but fair. Because I knew most of the tricks, having tried them myself as a kid, my students didn't get away with much.

The students I taught were mostly from working-class families. The usual temptations were waving at them: drugs, booze, sex, vandalism . . . You know, because it's the same stuff you may be dealing with. Instead of lecturing the students about these things (which would put them to sleep), I always tried to give them a game plan and a reason to resist self-destructive behavior.

Here's an example. There was an outbreak of graffiti at the school, and some of it was nasty sex stuff. "So-and-so is a whore" . . . garbage like that. This bad situation became contagious. Soon more than a few students were defacing school property with obscenities.

One day I walked into the classroom and told my students that the graffiti was pretty interesting. Immediately, I had everybody's attention. There were a few giggles. Then I dropped the truth bomb. I told them that the vandals who would write such crude sexual things on walls and desks had to be very immature sexually. They were probably frustrated and frightened by the topic of sex. I quoted a few sociologists who had done studies on sexual expression and concluded that graffiti is an attempt to combat sexual confusion. No more giggles. The classroom was dead silent.

Later that day, when I walked into the cafeteria, I realized that the place was buzzing with conversations about what I'd said. Also, some kids told me that a few of the graffiti artists were now being mocked as "sexually insecure." The vandalism ceased almost at once. Few teenagers want to be labeled as immature about sex.

Here is the lesson: Good teachers can and will instruct you about life and how to succeed. My students listened, then spread the word. You, too, must listen, and you must be open to asking the right questions. These men and women who teach you every day know a lot. But sometimes it's up to you to get it out of them.

I never had much patience with people who dismiss all teachers as incompetent or uncaring. That's foolish. But the really excellent teachers are rare, just as really excellent people are rare. Appreciate them when you find them.

If I had really wanted to make a career of teaching, I would have had to make a very strong commitment. I would have had to settle for modest financial expectations. I would have had to work nights and weekends, unpaid, to remain prepared.

I decided I couldn't make that kind of commitment. I was young and ambitious and, I guess, selfish. And I knew the job was too serious for me to do it halfheartedly. So I left teaching and began the long road to building a career in broadcasting.

If I had stayed, I probably would have done more harm than good, because my strongest ambitions lay elsewhere.

That may be true of some of your teachers.

But that's life.

You know how some people say that a bad winter is good because it makes you appreciate spring and summer all the more? When you have a weak teacher, try looking at it this way: he or she is only there to make you appreciate your smart, prepared, caring teachers even more. Be grateful that the good teachers are willing to make the financial sacrifice, to work hard, and to help you learn how to succeed in the world.

Just like cops and firemen and nurses, teachers are not given much respect by the movers and shakers of society. I know teachers who can deal with difficult students but have quit because rich, pushy parents interfere in the classroom, treating the teachers with contempt. Some parents respect only those they perceive to be powerful.

But you are getting mature enough to know better. Cherish a good teacher for what he gives you, and for what he's given up. There's power in what he or she has to impart. His life is already worthwhile because of the choice he's made, but it becomes even more worthwhile, I promise you, when you return his gift of teaching with the gift of doing your best in his class.

EYEWITNESS REPORT

I have to think like an adult even though I'm not, and yet still know my place as a teenager. So many people all day tell me, "You need to think of your future. These choices are going to affect you for the rest of your life." But as of now I'm keeping steady choosing my options and still keeping them open just in case I do grow into things I would never imagine I would like. I guess it's true that growing up was never said to be easy.

—*Brittany in New York*

I worry about what I want to do with my life. I have a few possibilities, but it seems so difficult to do any of them; I'm not sure I would be able to . . . I'm worried about what is going to happen to the rest of my life, and I am trying to figure it out.

—*Anne in Illinois*

It drives me crazy when I see and hear people slack off and observe that they don't give a damn about their future and will simply take it as it comes. I have a desire to do well in school, graduate from a good college, and do my absolute best to support myself, my future family, and in conjunction with those, my nation and its economy.

—*John in Connecticut*

Most of the other kids in my school think nothing of the future, wasting their life on drugs, sex, and brain-dead music and television. I realize that if this is what has become of my generation, what about my children? Are they going to grow up in the same environment as me? Or something worse?

—*Skye in Wisconsin*

MAKING
PLANS

Your teachers and parents, I bet, rag you all the time about the importance of having goals, getting your head focused, and making plans.

You want to know how smart I was about making plans?

Read this excerpt from a *Boston Globe* article about me published in November 1995. At the time, I had quit hosting a national TV program, *Inside Edition,* and was working to complete a master's degree at Harvard University:

> O'Reilly has post-school plans to travel to the Far East in January for a Harvard project. Beyond that, he's not sure where his next career move will take him. "I'll probably be driving a cab," he said.
>
> But he has no plans to go back to TV, unless things really change, he added. "In culture-shock terms, going from *Inside Edition* to doing homework at Harvard was like moving from Bangladesh to Beverly Hills; the gulf is so huge."

Ahem.

So much for my ability to predict my own future. Less than a year later, I was back in "Bangladesh," working to create the TV program that you know as *The Factor*. I am not driving a cab. Yet. And I did not travel to the Far East for a Harvard project.

So, does that mean your parents and teachers are wrong when they talk about the need to have goals and make plans? No.

Let me explain . . .

If someone else looks at the surface of my professional life, it might seem as if going from *Inside Edition* to Harvard postgraduate studies is wacko. But for me, that journey, even if not predictable, fit my long-term goals perfectly.

The secret to crafting a good plan involves one of my favorite words: balance.

Take two ideas and join them together . . .

1. **TO TAKE THE BEST ADVANTAGE OF LIFE'S OPPORTUNITIES, IT'S SMART TO SIT DOWN RIGHT NOW, IF YOU HAVEN'T ALREADY DONE THIS, AND LIST YOUR GOALS ON A PIECE OF PAPER.** Some of you may think that you don't have to do this because you already know what you want to do with your life. I know a jet pilot who knew he wanted to soar since the first time he saw a plane fly over his house when he was a kid. He stuck to his goal and today he still enjoys every assignment in the air.

But there's a possible danger in leaving no room for options. I also knew a kid who killed himself in high school after a bad fracture during a football game. He was determined to become a pilot, but the doctors said that his bones would never heal well enough for him to withstand the rigors of flight training in the U.S. Air Force. Although he was handsome, popular, and gifted, he proceeded to throw away his life because of one setback.

2. Which leads us to my second thought on the subject: **KEEP YOUR GOALS IN PERSPECTIVE . . . AND REMAIN FLEXIBLE.** That's the best way to stay in balance and on course. Let's say someone wants to be a fireman when he's very young. Then he decides in middle school that he wants to join the armed forces. Then in high school he decides he wants to become a doctor. Does that make him unstable? Of course not. In college, he might change his mind again. What he should look for is the thing that ties all of those goals together. Was he attracted to all of these possible jobs because they involve helping people? Does he see them all as offering adventure, or travel? Only he can answer that question, and only you can figure out why you choose your own goals. I repeat: attaining balance involves setting goals but also keeping flexible enough to revise them as your experience and circumstances change.

Something Abe Lincoln wrote sums it up best for me: "I will study and get ready and maybe someday my chance will come."

I've always interpreted old Abe's words to mean that you should work hard to control what you can control—study, practice, and discipline yourself—so that you will be ready to take advantage of the things you can't control, like great opportunities that seem to come out of nowhere. You don't win the *Teen Idol* contest by learning to sing in the shower the night before the auditions. You're not ready for a brand-new math scholarship that's just been set up by a generous benefactor unless you've been cracking the books for years.

So maybe my newspaper quote wasn't so whack after all.

At Harvard I was studying the field of public policy, trying to figure out how government can serve all of us effectively and honestly. That was my long-range goal. I did not have the specific goal of returning to television. I wasn't at all sure how I was going to use the knowledge I was gaining from my courses; I just concentrated on learning as much as possible and having fun with it.

Then the chance to create *The Factor* came, more or less, out of nowhere. A producer called, ideas were batted around, and suddenly I realized that my lifelong belief in the need for honest government could be used in a television program that would be original and important. With another nod to Abe, let me say that I had studied, I was ready . . . and my chance came.

I want that to happen to you.

You can make it happen.

Right now, list ten things you want to be when you're an adult. Think of things like "rich," "loved," "busy," "happy in my work," "married," and so forth. Arrange them in order of importance to you. If "mother of three" is the most important, make it number one on your list. If "different girl every weekend" is the most important goal, so be it. This list is just for you. I make no judgments.

Then date it and put it in a drawer. On the first of every month, look at the list. Does it need to be changed? Should you strike off some goals and add others? Is the order of importance still the same?

Do this every month for a while, and you may learn some amazing things about yourself. You will probably see big changes in your goals, because of what you've learned, the various kids you've met, and the many interactions you've had during each thirty-day period. Or you may discover that your ideas are pretty much set.

Earlier in this book, I stressed that I'd like to hear your reactions to what I have to say. Again, this is one of those times when I really want to know what you've learned (or didn't) by trying this simple exercise.

For fun, I tried it myself recently.

I was surprised.

So I guess I'm still studying and getting ready for the next great venture . . .

Pinheads and Smart Operators:

INSTANT MESSAGE Number 3

IMNSHO, **A Pinhead** gets sunburned. Okay, a nice even tan can make you look healthy and sexy. Or it can advertise to your friends that you've had a great winter vacation at the beach. But excessive sun exposure, according to the U.S. Army Office of the Surgeon General, can lead to skin cancer and other skin growths, cataracts, premature aging of the skin, and several other types of health problems. Heed the warnings! Boston University's Alan Geller led a study that found that only one-third of all twelve- to eighteen-year-olds in the United States use sunscreen. Many kids routinely suffer three or more sunburns every year. (Adults are no better; the Centers for Disease Control and Prevention found that nearly a third of adults get sunburned once a year. "There is no such thing as a safe tan," says a CDC researcher.) Tanning booths are just as bad, but you think they make you look good for the prom. Limit your exposure to the sun, use more sunscreen, or just learn to love your natural skin tone—any of these three options seems better to me than enduring a bad burn or worse.

A Smart Operator is a kid who is accepting of parental discipline. Okay, that's not easy to take, especially when you want to stay out late for a special concert or dance. "It's not fair!" you cry. But the shrinks tell us that deep down, kids feel safer when their parents establish guidelines and stick to them. (If the parents are wavering, it might be time for me to write an *O'Reilly Guide for Parents*.) Discipline gives you security. It gives you confidence. Sorry about the dance . . . there will be others. And you'll be ready for them when the time is right.

A Pinhead is a kid who is bored. Bored? Even if you don't live in the most exciting part of the world and don't have a gazillion bucks to spend on entertainment, you have more than almost anyone else did in all of history. You have gadgets, libraries, clubs, and sports teams. You have a community filled with activities and, most of all, you have a mind. A bored kid, I admit, is hard for me to understand. Look around. Think. Do something. Learn. If you're bored, you have only yourself to blame, which gets us nowhere. Forget the blame. Rev up your mind.

A Smart Operator is a kid who hugs his parents even at this age. Okay, do it when no one your age is looking . . . but do it. People thrive on being hugged. This is true in nurseries and in nursing homes. I know that all kinds of emotional turmoil and misunderstanding might be going on in your house right now. But is that a reason not to hug your father or mother? IDTS.

A Pinhead is a kid who makes fun of someone else for being "different," whatever that means. In the long run, the "different" types are likely to be more successful than the members of the herd, but that gives them little comfort when you're being cruel to them. Your brain is still forming. If you train it to practice cruelty, that behavior will lock in, and you will very likely lead a miserable life, devoid of the kind of loving relationships that enable one to thrive.

A Smart Operator is a kid who looks past her neighborhood, town, state, and country to see the world outside. On television, in magazines and newspapers, in some classes and in conversations with people who've traveled, you can learn about the variety of human life and behavior that exists on this huge planet. The more you learn, the more you understand yourself, your friends, and your family. IRMC. Listen up.

A Pinhead is a kid who finds a way to use the word "butt" in every other sentence, especially when shouting in the hallways at school. Sure, TV situation comedies rely on this word when the writers can't think of anything really funny. What can I say? It sounds stupid to me. SSINF.

THINGS TO
Think About

EYEWITNESS REPORT

Sleep. What many teenagers lack. Being an A student in every class, sleep is what is the biggest problem in my life and what seems many teenagers' lives. I get up at 5 A.M. for water polo practice, then have a rigorous day of school, trying to keep my eyelids open. Next follows three hours of practice after school, eating dinner, and showering, then hours of homework . . .

—*Tyler in California*

Women nowadays are shown in magazines and ads as tall, thin, and infallible . . . Only 8 out of every million women have a so-called "ideal" body type, and almost all models are airbrushed. Most models and actresses are anexoric or have some sort of eating disorder. I am definitely not saying that it is good to be obese, but I think you should be healthy, and being anorexic or throwing up food is not healthy.

—*Amanda in Oregon*

Bill, I'm 11 years old and I watch your show every night with my mom and stepdad, after I get back from the gym . . . My biggest problem is definitely my weight.

—*Kennedy in Georgia*

I pretty much have everything I could want, but I have bad eating habits (hot dogs, chips, and pop).

—*Amanda in Minnesota*

HEALTH

I wasn't always stupid in my teen years. Sometimes I did the smart thing . . . because I had no choice.

When I was growing up, we didn't have junk food available everywhere, certainly not in school. Even if we had, there wasn't enough spare change for me to indulge. A Coke was a treat, not an entitlement. Why buy candy several times a day when we had homemade desserts with meals at home?

So I couldn't, and didn't, break the first rule of good health: Keep the junk food under control.

Luckily, I also had a mad group of friends who were wild with unspent energy. If we weren't endangering our lives by climbing too high in trees, we played baseball and football. And we played hard. No one told us we should exercise. We just did it. I was surrounded by kids who liked running around like maniacs.

So I couldn't, and didn't, break the second rule of good health: Do something physical at least an hour a day. (Playing video games or using the TV remote doesn't count.)

If you break these rules, you are very likely to develop a body that becomes a burden. You're on the road to being overweight, and that's the road to bad health.

To quote Boston pediatrician Dr. Gerald Hass, "The combination of watching too much TV and eating junk food—if you'll pardon the pun—feeds itself."

Listen to me here: These are the things I'm NOT saying:

1. **I'M NOT SAYING THAT YOU ARE UNATTRACTIVE OR UNLIKABLE BECAUSE YOU ARE OVERWEIGHT.** Striving for what others call the ideal "body image" is not a sane reason for losing weight. We don't need a world of skinny anorexics.

2. **I'M NOT SAYING THAT IT WILL BE EASY TO CUT DOWN ON BAD FOOD AND START EXERCISING ON A REGULAR BASIS.** I am saying that bad food can be a short-term fix and that laziness can become habit-forming.

3. **MOST OF ALL, I'M NOT SAYING THAT YOU WILL BECOME WILDLY HAPPY WHEN YOU BEGIN TO EAT SMART AND EXERCISE SMART.** True, depression is associated with being overweight. Better health should make you feel better, but it's not the answer to all emotional problems. Better health is good for one simple reason: you're less likely to get sick.

Look around your classroom. An estimated one in six of your classmates is obese. Not fat, obese. That's what the medical experts say . . . and they're horrified.

What is obesity? According to *Merriam-Webster's Collegiate Dictionary,* it is "a condition characterized by the excessive accumulation and storage of fat in the body."

Gross?

Forget what it looks like. Think about what "excessive accumulation and storage of fat" is doing to your health.

Here are some clues:

In the last ten years, obesity in teenagers has tripled.

Doctors say that obesity is the most widespread and dangerous health problem for kids your age (and younger).

Obese teens are now getting diseases that used to be considered adult problems: clogged arteries, type 2 diabetes, high blood pressure.

Half of all obese teens will become obese adults.

Some people will blame your parents, your physicians, or your teachers for this growing problem. They argue that obesity should have been prevented in childhood.

But you and I, if you recall, have agreed that you are old enough to take responsibility for yourself. You're reading this book because you're too smart to play the blame game.

Besides, even if the school takes the junk food vending machines out of the corridors, you can easily find the stuff in other places.

If your parents closely monitor what you eat at home, you'll find junk food at a friend's house or at the movies.

If your parents pressure you to exercise, you'll hate every second of it, and that's the wrong approach.

As for schools, forget it. I was amazed to learn that two out of three high schools in America do not require teens to go to a gym class every day. (Do they want to kill you?)

So, it's up to you.

And it won't be easy.

Let me say again, I was lucky. By the time junk food overran the world, I was in college and had no taste for the stuff. I sometimes walk down the aisles of a supermarket today and am bewildered. You have to pass rows and rows of products before you find something that can honestly be called "food." Nasty orange puffs in big cellophane bags, fizzy sodas in gallon-size plastic bottles—this is not food. Anything that has a "sell-by" date of a decade or more is not good for you. Big Gulps are big trouble.

I once saw a hefty young mother with two young children at the checkout counter. Her shopping cart was stacked high with packaged foods. The children had already broken open a carton and were munching on the junk. I just knew they had a long afternoon and evening of watching TV instead of any fun physical activity.

Now, I repeat: I'm not making fun of the overweight mother because of her looks. I'm saying that her practices are endangering her children's future health. All of the physicians agree that it is much harder to reverse unhealthy weight gains in the teenage years than earlier in childhood.

So what can you do?

Try this . . .

1. **DON'T GO OVERBOARD.** Make one change at a time. Cut down on junk food; don't cut it out entirely. Substitute fresh fruit occasionally, not three times a day. Don't immediately start drinking eight glasses of water a day. Start with one or two.

2. **ASK YOUR PHYSICIAN TO CHECK YOUR BMI.** This is your *body mass index*. It tells you how much body fat is healthy for you at your age and height. Make him or her understand that you are serious. A good physician will then work with you to devise a diet and exercise program that will be right for you. By the way, you may need to explain that you're not thinking about "body image" but rather about good health. (That may give your doctor a heart attack right there.)

3. **CHOOSE THE RIGHT KIND OF EXERCISE.**

   Something fun . . .

   And start slowly.

   When you're at the mall or in your apartment building, take the stairs instead of using the elevator or escalator. Park away from wherever you're going so that you have to walk some distance. Get off the bus or subway ten blocks early.

Take lessons, like swimming or tennis. (You're not "exercising," you're learning something.) You may not have the money or access to some kinds of exercise, so be creative.

4. LEARN TO COOK. When you cook for yourself you can choose what to eat, you can make sure it's healthy, and you'll probably have fun, too. I grew up in an Irish-American family where the men never learned to cook. I'm always jealous of an Italian-American friend who was taught to cook by his father and can make anything. A good cook can always take care of himself. (Or make a lot of money in the restaurant business.)

Finally, don't blame yourself if your weight is unhealthy. Just get on with the future. Your goals should be to eat healthful food, to engage in an hour of physical activity every day, and to limit sedentary pastimes—viewing no more than two hours of TV or playing no more than two hours of video games a day.

When it all starts to kick in, you'll thank me.

And I have you to thank. Writing this reminds me that I've been letting all of this sitting at the computer and at the radio and TV stations settle around my middle lately.

See ya at the track . . .

EYEWITNESS REPORT

I recently have gotten a second job to save up for a car, which I need to get to and from work. I pay for my own clothes, school, insurance, lunch, and all the other things in my life. What is appalling is the kids that receive all of these things for free from their parents, while I work hard to manage half of these things.

—*John in Wisconsin*

WORK

I t looks easy, doesn't it?

Well, it's supposed to . . . because I work hard at making it look easy.

Maybe you turn on the TV or switch on the radio and there I am, hammering away off the top of my head. I'm not looking at notes. I'm not reading questions. You don't see an aide handing me a cheat sheet (as if I were a congressman holding a hearing without a clue).

But what you're seeing is only the surface of things.

I want to talk about work because unless you're going to inherit a lot of money or marry into a family that has lots of it, work will be the key to making a successful life for yourself.

Work gives you two things:

1. **MONEY, SO THAT LIFE IS NOT A DRAG, AND**
2. **FULFILLMENT, SO THAT YOU ENJOY WHAT YOU DO AND CAN FEEL THAT YOUR LIFE MEANS SOMETHING.**

These two things are vital to your well-being.

When you do your best on an exam, you're learning how to work, because you've organized your time, studied, and thought about things.

When you make an athletic team or get cast in a part in the school play or join a band, you will just be beginning to learn how to work. That means learning to work with others. That means coming to practice or rehearsal fully prepared. That means learning to go off by yourself to work on things you're not yet doing well. That means learning how to listen to advice. Unless you're different from most people, it also means learning how to deal with failure . . . by starting all over again.

Back to me for a minute: I don't want to tell you how much I work, because then I'd be bragging. But I want to prepare you for reality, and examples can help do that.

Every weekday morning I get up at 7:00 A.M. and read several newspapers so that I can absorb what's going on in the world. Then I write a TV or newspaper commentary giving my opinion on some recent event. Easy? You try writing three pages every day, no matter how you feel. After that, I start planning my radio and TV programs. I talk with my staff by phone about setting up interviews. After that I leave home for the TV studios in Manhattan, where I will write the entire script for *The O'Reilly Factor.* I'll also begin preparing my questions and approaches to the topics that will be discussed on my daily two-hour radio program. Off and on during the day, I will prepare to interview the four or five guests who will be on my nightly hour-long TV program. Some of them will be hostile, so I'll want to be sure I've anticipated every argument and have researched my points well. Along the way, I might deal with agents, editors, lawyers, and others involved in my books. The radio program is live on the air from 12:00 P.M. to 2:00 P.M. Just before 6:00 P.M. I go to the TV studio to host *The Factor.* Sometime after 7:00 P.M., unless there's a special nightly program because of some breaking news, I head toward home and my family.

How do I spend weekends? Writing and delivering speeches, writing my books, reading some more, and watching news so that I am always prepared.

I repeat: I'm not bragging. I'm just telling you how it is.

And I'm sure not complaining. Success is great—and the best revenge against those who didn't believe in me before now.

But it didn't happen overnight.

As your parents know from having read my previous books, I spent a very long time learning how to become a success. I made so many mistakes you'd need a semester to read about them all. Even five years ago, I was not a household name. Publishers did not believe that a book of mine would be a bestseller. Politicians did not believe that it was important to accept an invitation to appear on my program.

All of that has changed.

But none of this "overnight success" could have happened if I had given up and decided to slack off. I'm here because I never stopped working, never stopped trying to learn.

I want you to apply my story to your everyday life.

Whenever you make a lower grade than you want, remind yourself that it took O'Reilly decades to get where he is. Maybe, with a little more work, thought, and concentration, it will take you only a few weeks to improve your grades.

Did you drop the ball? Forget a line onstage? Hit the wrong chord? Remember, you can deal with all of these challenges in less time than it took O'Reilly to get where he is today, if you try.

I bet you've noticed a couple of things in this chapter:

1. **I'M ASSUMING THAT YOU DO THINGS.** I can't very well give advice about work to the couch potato eating Pringles, can I? (A couch potato eating Pringles sounds vaguely like cannibalism, doesn't it?)

2. I KEEP USING WORK AS A GOOD WORD. English teachers call it a **PURR** word. I guess that you know too many adults who use it as a **SNARL** word.

You know why? Because they're doing something they hate. I want you to learn how to work so that you can do work that keeps you alert and alive.

Like me.

How many hours did you spend practicing jump shots last night? If you know, you were working with the wrong attitude.

How many hours did you spend studying last night? If you were enjoying it too much to count, then you were working with the right attitude.

Keep it up.

My Story:

Work is an interesting concept. We should be proud to do it, but some of us are not. We should understand that hard work defines a person just as sitting around on your butt does. I know middle-aged men and women who've lost their high-paying jobs but won't take a lower-paying job because it would be "embarrassing." That's stupid. Honest work is always admirable. I have worked ever since I was able to.

When I was a young kid, my father made me cut the lawn. At first I hated it. But then I learned something . . . as I got pretty good at it, other people paid me to cut their lawns. That meant money for the movies and stuff.

Then I began shoveling snow in the winter and babysitting on weekends. More cash meant more freedom! No more asking the folks for money and having them want to know how I was going to spend it. Right?

At age sixteen I started working in an ice cream store. Great job. Lots of fun, a little money . . . and I could give free cones to pretty girls. Soon, however, I realized that fast food was slow cash. I decided to start my own business, painting houses. I did this for five summers and made big bucks, enough to do pretty much anything I wanted and also save money for college.

Even while teaching high school in Florida I supplemented my income by becoming a bouncer at the Wreck Bar in Miami Beach. After that, I went to grad school at Boston University, but I also wrote freelance articles and drove a cab part-time.

I was always working and learning at the same time. This very strong work ethic has prepared me for what I do today and has brought me success and big money. Hard work rules!

Don't forget that.

It's a primary rule of life.

EYEWITNESS REPORT

People in my school and generally people in my age group throw around the "n" word. I am very antiracism and it makes my blood boil when I hear people calling each other the "n" word.

—Rebecca in New Jersey

I and all of my fellow teens are always stereotyped as hooligans and generally bad people. In malls, security always has one eye on teens, and if you look the least bit suspicious, they will stop you and search your bag . . . This is an outrage.

—Max in Illinois

All the popular kids are just judgmental human beans. I happen to hang out with the punks, who don't really care what people think of them. We are always asked about what we look like and why we wear what we wear. All it is, is cheap vintage clothes. I think that judgment shouldn't even exist on this earth.

—Dana

People who are different usually get beat up, picked on, humiliated, have rumors going around about them, etc. Some people are even favored more than others depending on race, ethnic background, religion, sexual orientation, weight, and even what social group they're in. People should stop jumping to conclusions and get to know people before they judge them. The whole world would be a better place that way.

—Crystal in Pennsylvania

Usually my biggest problem is people judging me before they get to know me. I hate it so much! Though I usually deal with it just fine . . .

—Natalie in Ohio

STEREOTYPES

You hear this word all the time, but don't yawn . . . because I don't think you really know where it comes from. In printing years ago, a stereotype was a kind of mold for letters or a picture. Cover it with ink and it produced the same image over and over again. Each copy would be the same as all the others. As long as the mold didn't break, you could make all the copies you wanted to, each one alike.

That's the idea behind "stereotyping" other people. The stupidest kind of stereotyping, of course, is racism, but there are many other kinds, too.

Before we talk about them, let me give you the first argument against stereotypes: it's right there in the mirror. It's you . . .

Do you consider yourself an exact copy of anyone else in the world? You do not. You think you are a unique individual. You are right.

Do the math. If you're the only you, so is everyone else. That's true even though there are six billion people alive right now. Have you ever met anyone who is exactly like anyone else you know? You have not. Even identical twins and triplets are different from each other.

You've heard about cloning. Perhaps it will be possible one day to make a copy of your genes and manufacture a baby with exactly the same genetic structure as yours. But will that child be you? No way. It will have different parents, eat different foods, know different friends, learn from different teachers—and in all other ways become a different person from you because of the different experiences and influences it will encounter.

So here's the conclusion: every human being is unique.

Which of the following is also true?

1. AFRICAN AMERICANS **CANNOT** LEARN TO PILOT PLANES.
2. JEWISH AMERICANS **CANNOT** PLAY BASEBALL.
3. WOMEN **CANNOT** LEARN TO BECOME PHYSICIANS.
4. CHINESE AMERICANS ARE **CARRIERS** OF BUBONIC PLAGUE.
5. MEN ARE **INCAPABLE** OF CARING FOR BABIES.
6. ITALIAN AMERICANS ARE **ALL** OVERWEIGHT.

The above are all false. But these are all stereotypes that were widely believed by people of my parents' generation. Many people didn't question such stupid ideas because of ignorance, because of the need to feel superior to another group of human beings, or because of fear of people who looked or sounded different.

Do you believe any of the stereotypes you hear today?

If you do, now is the time for you to begin thinking for yourself.

First of all, think about where stereotypes come from. If all people of a certain race or ethnic group live in the same neighborhood, it is natural that they may develop shared habits of behavior. If you are white and live in the suburbs, do you agree that "all white people have lawn mowers"? If you are middle-class and live in a city, do you agree that "all middle-class people live in a building with a doorman"?

Those comments are stupid. So is any other stereotype you might hear. You can bet I'm right.

Since race is always lurking under the surface of this subject, let's do a little experiment. No matter what your racial or ethnic background, write down the names of ten Caucasians you know and ten African Americans you know. If you don't have friends who fit the bill, look at a sports or entertainment person instead.

I'm serious. Put down this book and make those lists.

Okay. I hope you're playing along with me . . . Now visualize the people on your lists. At first glance you have two very different groups of people: ten people of color, ten "white" people.

But let's look at these human beings from another point of view. Suppose you were a Martian trying to figure out Earth's various groups. What would keep you from classifying all of the tall people as one "race"? Or all of the stocky people as another? Or all of the people who play sports as different from those who make music? Or the people who laugh a lot as different from those who are very studious?

Are you with me yet?

There's no reason to group people by skin color when there are so many other characteristics that either bind us together or make us unique. Looking at someone's outside is just a very arbitrary, bad, dangerous social habit.

Certain parts of your own personality have been influenced by your family, friends, and neighbors. If you're all from the same ethnic background, that might mean you eat similar foods or wear similar clothes. But, as you know, there is as much variety within your ethnic group as there is within any other ethnic group.

Unfortunately, not everyone is on the same page with me here. It's just not how many people think. But it's the smart way to think, because it's the truth.

Stereotypes are stupid.

They're for lazy people.

If you want to understand the human beings around you better—and that's part of the fun of life—remember that they are just like you in at least one way: each one is unique.

And remember one more thing . . . Americans of every race, color, and creed are now targets of people who believe some stereotype about us. We are all in this together. Al Qaeda doesn't care what you look like . . . they will kill you because you're an American. If that doesn't unite us, nothing will.

EYEWITNESS REPORT

Our Halloween party was not allowed to be a Halloween party. It had to be a "fall party" because two kids in my class do not believe in Halloween because of their religion. My mom says they did this because it was "politically correct." I think it stinks.

— *Maria in Ohio*

I worry about what will happen with Social Security when my generation hits middle age. Our numbers simply cannot support such a large baby-boomer generation.

— *William in California*

Those darn Democrats want to sacrifice our freedoms for peace. Yeah, I like peace, too, and I wish the world was at peace, but it's not going to happen anytime soon . . . Our entire country is founded on the basis of equality and liberty for all. That goes for the Iraquis, too.

— *J G*

Why do you support President Bush when he is misinforming the people about tax cuts and WMDs in Iraq? Any American could figure out that the tax cuts mostly give money back to the rich, and the WMDs in Iraq are nonexistent.

— *Nicolas in California*

American children are not thankful for their freedom, because they don't understand it. They do not realize that freedom means being able to worship however you please or speak out against whatever you want, though most Americans exercise these rights every day. In my opinion, this lack of gratitude is a disgrace.

— *Lauren in Washington*

I don't understand all the political conflicts going on in the world. I like your GOOD sense of humor. You make politics easier to understand.

— *Danny*

POLITICS

Some people would define politics as boring old people lying to the public, stealing money, and fighting with each other.

If that's your definition, I can't blame you.

That's pretty much what you see on television.

But the truth is more complex than that. These people have the power to change your life in dramatic ways.

You can't vote now, but you can begin to learn how positive or how dangerous that power can be. It's important to understand and be involved in politics—for your own protection. It's how hard-working, fair-playing citizens preserve the right to live the good life they deserve. And if you think politics has no role in your day-to-day life at school, you're wrong.

If you are a member of a minority group attending a school where many races are represented, you've been affected by politics. If Congress, under pressure from a president, had not passed civil rights legislation, you would not be allowed in your school. Hard to believe? Well, it's true. Look it up.

If you are a girl playing sports with good equipment, professionally trained coaches, and a full competitive schedule during the school year, you've been affected by politics. If Congress had not passed Title IX legislation, there would be less money to support your female-oriented sports program. Hard to believe? It's true. Ask your teachers.

If your music program was canceled this year because there was not enough money from local taxes to keep it going, that's also due to politics, pure and simple.

In each of these cases, elected officials in your community or far away in Washington, D.C., made decisions that have and will continue to influence your life every day you live it.

Think about that.

Is it a scary thought?

Not really.

What's scary is that so few people (and I include the nearly 50 percent of all adults who do not vote in elections) understand the power of politics. Worse, they do not take responsibility for what results from their inactivity.

I'm not going to rant here about freedom and the right to vote and the history of tyranny. Those are good subjects, but I leave them to your history teachers.

I'm just talking about the facts of life.

The kind of politics you say you're not interested in (the kind involving boring old people making speeches) actually begins in your schoolyard. Look at the kids who are elected to school office. Study them, even if you are one of them. Do they get elected because of their good looks? Their big wide grins? Their brains? Or because of promises they've made, kept, or broken? As I said, study them well. Many of these types, for better or for worse, are going to be running for office when you're an adult, and you have to learn to tell whether or not they have your best interests at heart.

In fact, there's politics of many different kinds, all around you at school. The kids who know how to get what they want from a teacher today may end up as the weasel in the office who knows exactly how to get around your boss tomorrow. That person gets how office politics works.

And what about the kids who never seem to take the blame for anything that goes wrong—the kids who always get away with cheating, stealing, or telling a lie about you behind your back? How do they do it? They know a little something about politics, too. They can fool others easily. You will meet such people throughout the rest of your life. They'll be filing false insurance claims, trying to sell you something you don't need, or overcharging you for some service rendered.

This all sounds pretty negative.

But it doesn't have to be.

Good people can use their political skills for good ends, too. One of your school leaders can get the rest of you to support change that's good for the school. A naturally skilled young politician can stick up for a kid who's being teased and change the climate of the classroom. A good politician will use the looks, the grin, and the political gift along with a positive agenda to change things for the better.

Learn the difference now, and you may be able to make smart political decisions in the future.

If you've ever watched *The O'Reilly Factor,* you know that I spend a lot of time on political subjects. That's because I know that politics can mean so much in the life of the average American. If taxes are raised, what does that do to your family's ability to live comfortably? You have to learn these things. If the government does not protect you from drug dealers and other criminals, what can you do about it? What is going to happen to your grandparents if their medicines get so expensive that they can't pay for them?

These are all questions that are addressed by politicians. What they do depends upon your involvement when you are old enough to vote, but you can begin preparing for that responsibility right now.

Most experts will tell you that teenagers are likely to back the same political leaders as their parents.

Nothing's wrong with that, as long as you're thinking for yourself. Are you?

If not, now's the time to start.

Lastly, don't make the mistake of hanging out only with people who agree with you. As Yale College dean Richard Brodhead asked the incoming freshmen at the start of the 2003 school year, "Who do we suppose will be able to deal more constructively with the challenges of our time: people who have only ever experienced preaching to the converted, or people who tested their understanding against the countervailing understandings of others?" I hope you agree that the answer is obvious.

And who knows? The more you explore, the more you may discover that you like politics and you may even decide to run for office someday. And that's good. We need good people like you.

EYEWITNESS REPORT

Recently, my boyfriend was in a car crash and died instantly. All that knew him have been affected deeply . . . If you were to walk into a high school, you would hear almost all conversations dealing with who is dating who, but my problem is dealing with the death of my best friend and boyfriend.

—Ayla in California

My biggest problem is getting along with my mom since my father died last year. It's really hard for me and for her, because our personalities clash.

—Stormy in Mississippi

DEATH

Many of us experience the loss of a loved one for the first time in our lives during our teen years. It may be an older relative, neighbor, or family friend who dies. It may be another teen who has lost control of his car and has come to a violent end. That's when we notice that the clock of our mortality is ticking. As a famous French writer, Madame de Staël, once said, "We understand death for the first time when he puts his hand upon one whom we love."

Is it crazy to think about death and what it means?

Absolutely not.

The trick is to try to understand it without becoming obsessed about it.

Some people think that we can't really understand life without trying to understand death.

Clue Number 1: No one has the complete answer. If someone tells me that she knows the secret to eternal life, I might listen, but I'm not necessarily going to buy into her theory. I'm the kind of person who has to figure these things out for myself. Try figuring things out for yourself, too. Look at nature, at religion, at great writing . . . Talk with your family, friends of all ages, mentors. Develop your own answers to your questions on this profound subject.

Clue Number 2: We're all in the same boat. When you first begin to think deep thoughts about death, you might think you discovered the problem for the first time! Think again. Every human being throughout the ages has worried and wondered about death. That's what makes us different from all other living creatures. We know that we will die. We can't change that. What we can do is choose how to deal with that knowledge.

Clue Number 3: Yes, the death of a loved one can make us sad. The hurt can last for a very long time. But we do heal. After a while, we remember the good, and move forward. The loss of one person should make us realize how much the living means to us. Death, though it hurts, shows us how wonderful life is. A part of you will never forget the death of someone you love. But you realize that he or she would want you to get on with your life and continue to love others.

Clue Number 4: Do not brood about death. And seek help for a friend or acquaintance who does. If you let thoughts of death get you down too much, you could be headed into a very dangerous depression. Don't keep your worries to yourself. Don't be so "strong" you won't let yourself cry. Face your feelings. Fear of death should not make you afraid to live. Feeling grief is not a sign of weakness. It shows how much you are able to love.

My Story:

When I was thirteen, my grandfather died. I saw him lying there in the casket, his hands folded over his stomach, his eyes closed. He was a good guy, but he seemed very old to me. My reaction to his parting was based more on curiosity about death than any other reaction or feeling. I never really dwelled on it.

But that was a mistake. I should have thought about it more. Maybe if I had I wouldn't have gone on to do some of the life-threatening things I did—like scuba diving without a buddy, wing-walking on top of a rickety propeller plane for a TV story (the single dumbest thing I have ever done), or driving thousands of miles cross-country without sufficient rest. (For the record, fatigued driving can be as dangerous as drunken driving, in case you didn't know.) Like you, I thought I was invincible.

But then a strange thing happened: Some of my friends started to die. First, Paul Hanly drowned while serving in the Merchant Marine. Then Danny Callahan drowned while swimming in the Atlantic Ocean. Clement Simonetti was found dead from some rare malady I still can't understand. A few neighborhood guys got shot up in Vietnam. Suddenly death was a factor in my life.

And it should be one in yours, too . . . to this extent: Respect your life and the lives of all others, including unborn children. Realize that you have only one life, so you have an obligation to live it honestly and with vigor! Have a lot of fun, accomplish many things, and associate with good people. My last book, *Who's Looking Out for You?,* deals with those themes. If you like this book, you might want to check that one out, too.

In the end, death is something over which you have no control. When your time is up, it's up. All of the whining in the world will not change that. So accept the reality that you will someday be lying there just like my grandfather. (I hope it's when you are good and old just like him.) And remember that death is not to be feared, because that does no good at all. Fear is a total waste of time. Instead, make death a motivator: as long as you're breathing, be as alive as you can be. Live a good life—a decent, generous, active, fun, worthwhile life.

By the way, silly people do not understand how some kinds of reactions help us all learn more about death.

Suppose a rock star or famous ballplayer or popular actor suddenly dies. Thousands of fans may express their grief publicly, while silly people sneer, "They didn't even know the person." But that's not the point. Fans may be sincerely grieving for a loss in their emotional lives. Even someone admired or loved from a distance can be important to you as a role model or symbol. Loss is loss, and only you can know what you've lost. You can't just turn off those feelings. It's not healthy.

Some silly people may even make fun when someone cries over the death of a pet. Trust me, you're never too old to grieve for a beloved pet. If you've done your part well, then you've fed, played with, groomed, and walked this companion for years. You're a better person if you've learned how to live responsibly with your pet. You've made an emotional connection that is, for many people, an important part of growing up. You can't just turn away and say, "Well, it was just an animal." That's not human.

At times of death many people are often at a loss for words of comfort or may even say the wrong thing unintentionally. "It's good that she died; she was in so much pain/so old/so out of it." When people say these things, they surely mean well. They want to help you accept your loss. Be grateful for their care and concern, but you must still let yourself grieve in your own way. Grief is not only normal, it is healthy.

Grief counselors believe that we all go through stages of grief but that the pattern is different for each of us. Shock, numbness, insomnia, uncontrolled weeping, anger, physical pangs, fatigue, depression, even hallucinations—these reactions are not unusual.

But remember, you have to express your grief in the way that works best for you. When I was in my teens, a friend's father died of cancer. At the wake, I heard some kid say, "Joe must not have liked his father; he isn't crying." I hope you know that was a foolish thing for him to say. We can't know how someone else is dealing with their grief. Some people will not or cannot show their emotions in public; others will weep and wail. It's not for you and me to judge. As it happens, I knew that my friend was dazed with grief. He remembers his father with love to this day. No one will ever know the depth of his pain.

Has this been a depressing chapter?

Well, it shouldn't be.

Death is a reality. As I've tried to say before, being a teenager is both exciting and challenging because you are facing things you could not handle very well as a young child. You're growing up. Sometimes you may want to draw back, because life may seem too puzzling or difficult. But you'll get back in the race, I know, because you will want to understand things for yourself in your own way.

That's the smart way to run your life, and as far as death is concerned, don't fear it. Live well, do exciting and worthwhile things, be a force for good. Then when you are in your last days, you'll be content. A life well lived is the most worthwhile goal on this earth.

EYEWITNESS REPORT

The biggest problem in my life would be trying to keep a close relationship with God in a world of such madness, when just about everyone says there is no God.

— *Kendall in Texas*

The major problem I have encountered growing up as a 13-year-old in America is having faith. That basic faith in God is the only way I can get through the day. It's what lets me deal with the chaos of growing up.

— *Erin in Florida*

GOD . . . ?

When it comes to the mysteries of religion, I have no right to tell you what to believe.

That works both ways: you have no right to tell me—or anyone else—what to believe.

You might present the case for your religious belief. I can listen . . . or not. But you can't force me to believe what you believe, or to change my beliefs. In America, religious freedom is absolute.

Talking about different beliefs, Abe Lincoln once said, "Whatever you are, be a good one."

At this time of your life, your brain and heart and soul are no doubt reaching out to explore ideas that the younger you probably never even thought about.

You might be asking . . .

Is there a God?

What does He (or She!) want from me?

Will I continue to exist after death?

Can religion make me happy?

Am I alive for a reason?

If you aren't asking some of these questions and others like them, I don't think that you are fully responding to life and its mysteries.

Of course, you may feel that you know all of the answers, because you were raised in a certain faith and remain loyal to that faith. If so, that's fine. But I can tell you that it is the rare human being who does not continually reexamine these questions of faith throughout his or her life.

Or you may feel that religion has no place in your life and never will.

Okay, but let me tell you what religion has meant to me. This is just a personal conversation. I'm not preaching. I'm sharing.

I was raised as a Catholic and went to an all-boys Catholic high school. So, was I a saint? How about a hellion?

I was the same loudmouth you see today. I was no shrinking violet in my high school years. You've probably seen my type in a movie—a very bad comedy. I made life difficult for nuns and priests alike—not out of pure meanness, but because I insisted on questioning things. How did they know that the beliefs of the Catholic Church made sense? I wanted explanations! And I wanted them now!

In my school, teenage boys participated in the Catholic Mass as altar boys. How innocent we looked in our white vestments! How pious, how devout we seemed as we performed various rites while the priest chanted and the choir sang!

The truth was very different, however. We were all hellions before and after services. I wasn't one of those guys who got tipsy on the ceremonial wine, but I did some other pretty weird things.

My Story:

My career as an altar boy began at age eleven. I had no choice in the matter; my mother made me do it. So I memorized the prayers and tried my best. The downside was that Mass was said at 6:30 A.M. The upside was that we altar boys made money at weddings and funerals.

Now, I've already told you that I always worked. To me, this altar boy gig was an extension of that ethic. On Saturdays weddings were often held at St. Brigid's Church. Two altar boys usually assisted the priest. The best man was expected to tip the boys. If the tip was not forthcoming, he and I would have the following chat:

ME: Excuse me, sir. Are you the best man?

GUY: That's me, son.

ME: Well, I just want to thank you for tipping Father Murphy so generously . . . but you may not know that Father does not share his good fortune with his assistants.

GUY: I didn't know that.

ME: And it's really too bad, because Richie and I will be holding the plates [with the chalice of wine and the host] during the ring ceremony . . . and that takes strength and stamina [Here I looked the guy straight in the eye], if you know what I mean.

GUY: [after slight pause] Here's a ten for the two of you.

Extortion? Come on. Enterprise is more like it. We altar boys did all the setup and cleanup while Father Murphy got the glory. My "explanation" was only fair, and as you may know, "God helps those who help themselves."

You might ask, what did any of this have to do with belief in God?

Well, slowly, as I finally began to mature, I began to understand what the regular church services, the religious instruction, and the dedication of certain (by no means all) priests was teaching me.

I began to see that the religious texts were not just ancient words . . . They were the writings of people who had asked questions about faith just as I was beginning to do.

I began to learn that going to services on a regular basis gave me a kind of timeout from all the turmoil of my teenage years . . . For that hour or so, if I wanted to, I could think about the challenges of life and wonder what it all meant.

I began to appreciate the sense of community . . . Here we were, people of all ages and different backgrounds, united for a while in considering the mysteries of existence.

I began to recognize the great beauty of religious music and art . . . They had survived over the ages because they provided peace and joy and inspiration.

Surely these are the kinds of things that all religions give to people. If you aren't interested in such things, I'd be surprised.

Did the Church give me all the answers? No way.

Has the Church, because of bad leadership, disappointed me? Yes.

Have the sex scandals that surfaced recently destroyed the lives of many? Definitely.

Has organized religion, when practiced by lunatics, led to wars and terrorism throughout the centuries? Yes.

But I don't confuse any single religion with the need to understand what life is all about. A religion is going to be partly a human creation, and humans are flawed.

Yet one of our strongest virtues, I think, is the very human yearning to find a meaning in our lives.

If you are feeling that yearning, I believe that you are lucky, no matter what answers you come up with.

Some religious questions are very troubling:

Why do tragedies happen to very good people?
Why isn't life fair?
Why is an innocent child born with a life-threatening or horribly disfiguring illness?

Believe me, people of faith have been struggling with these questions for a very long time.

For me, the father of two young children, there are also the more positive questions that arise every day. How could such perfectly formed little creatures exist, born with tiny working fingers and eager bright eyes and questioning brains?

Is it just chance?
Were they created by a Divine Power?
What gave them such miraculous life?

To repeat, I don't have the answers, although I have my suspicions. After all, we human beings can build huge cities, send probes to Mars, and split the atom. But we cannot create even a single atom, even a single atomic particle, out of nothing.

I think life will be richer for you if you think about such things, discuss them with your friends or family, and always, always keep an open mind.

I mean, you do not want to be like the mean-spirited, self-righteous religious maniacs who attack me when I say something that sets them off. If you watch *The Factor,* you may have heard me read one of these angry letters or e-mails at the end of the program.

Suggest that people of all races have the same rights and responsibilities in a democracy? They hang garlic around their necks and exclaim that O'Reilly is more dangerous than Dracula.

Speculate that decent, hard-working gays might make good adoptive parents? The bigots foam at the mouth. You can hear the sizzle of O'Reilly being turned on a spit in the depths of Hell (in their imaginations).

If your faith makes you angry and scared and unmerciful, it doesn't pass the religion tests I mentioned earlier. Faith should be a living force, a way for you to shape a good, caring life for yourself.

Faith never means that I'm always right, or you're always right, or any religious leader is always right.

We're human.

That's why some of us believe that we need God.

You may not. But the choice, in this society, is always yours.

Yet I can tell you that God has never let me down. I pray one prayer: "Please allow me to use my talents for good." That prayer has been answered over and over again. When times were tough in my life, I knew they would get better. I took the pain, and things did get better. To this day I continue to pray. Somebody is listening to me. That's what I, for one, firmly believe.

EYEWITNESS REPORT

There are not enough people my age acting responsible. And they don't help others enough.

—*Nick in Pennsylvania*

HELPING
OTHERS

F inancial success has meant three things to me, most of all. I think you're going to be surprised by what those things are.

In the first place, my financial success has meant that I can provide my family a safe, comfortable home with access to good schools, clean parks and playgrounds, and decent neighbors. That's Job One, in my book, for any parent. It's not easy and I'm grateful I can do it.

Second, my financial success has helped to buy me freedom, freedom to say what I want to, even if a powerful person in government or business or entertainment doesn't like it. They can't hurt me. Money protects me from their schemes. I have always said what I think, but because of financial security I don't have to worry that I am jeopardizing my family's welfare whenever I make a powerful person mad.

The third thing may surprise you.

It kind of surprised me at first. And that's how great it feels to be able to use my money to help others. I'm not making that up. I'm not bragging about my sensitivity. It's just the plain truth.

I've been able to help kids in bad family situations. How could I not enjoy doing that, when I see how lucky I am? Why would I spend money on Hummers, vacation homes, or fancy dinners every night when that's just overconsumption in my book? I don't need the newest gadgets or a huge wardrobe. I don't need to buy a few pieces of expensive fine art; I can go to museums and see hundreds of masterpieces. I don't have to display my money.

But I enjoy seeing what I can do to help worthy people and worthwhile organizations.

It's a habit that you can start now, even if you don't have piles of money. It's a habit that will enrich your life.

I've got some ideas, but you may have better ones:

1. **SET ASIDE A CERTAIN AMOUNT OF MONEY FOR A GROUP YOU SUPPORT.** Some people believe in giving 10 percent of their income to good causes. You make your own decision. Then stick to it. If you slack off one month because you need the new Avril Lavigne CD, you're not keeping your word to yourself.

2. **MONEY ISN'T EVERYTHING.** If you can't give financial support to a good cause, you can volunteer. Look around in your community to find out which groups need help. You're old enough to participate in fund drives or answer telephones. And helping out others also helps you. In the process you'll probably learn that there are people out there who have much worse problems than you do. You'll probably make friends you wouldn't meet otherwise. You'll develop confidence in dealing with strangers, with older people, or with kids from very different backgrounds than yours.

3. **VISIT OR HELP SOMEONE WHO HAS PROBLEMS.** I've already talked about spending time with the elderly, but what about a kid you know who is wheelchair-bound? Or needs help

learning to read better? You're not going to be much good if you feel sorry for someone like that. But if you have the right attitude, both of you will benefit. Helping someone else is one of life's greatest pleasures. If you don't think so, I bet you haven't tried it.

Of course, not everyone reacts with gratitude when you want to help, but that's just another life lesson that will prepare you for the adult world. Some people will think that your kindness is pity, and they won't want any part of it. Bad things make some people crabby; they want to be left alone. Don't let yourself be hurt by that kind of attitude. If you know that you mean well, that's what really counts.

My Story:

A friend of mine felt very uneasy around kids who had been labeled mentally retarded. She was afraid she couldn't understand what they said. She was nervous when they openly showed their emotions.

Then a couple whose young daughter had Down's syndrome moved into her neighborhood. My friend was friendly but distant. To her amazement, her own children became good friends with the little girl and began inviting her home to play. (Hint: Her own children were too young to have developed any biases against the girl's condition.)

Slowly, my friend, who is a kind and understanding woman, also came to love this little girl. She saw beyond the surface behavior. She responded to the girl's enthusiasm and laughter and innocent affection. Eventually my friend became deeply involved in special sports programs for kids with this condition.

This kind of thing can happen when you take time on a regular basis to look outside yourself and try to give something back to the world, whether it's money or time or both. I don't think it matters which good cause you support; it matters that you do something.

Trying to make the world a better place for other people is the smart thing to do. It helps them and it helps you.

Pinheads and Smart Operators:

INSTANT MESSAGE Number 4

A Pinhead does not wear a seat belt. According to a survey of New England high schools taken by the Insurance Institute for Highway Safety, fewer than half of you wear seat belts, even when your parents are driving you somewhere and they are wearing seat belts. And when an adult driver is stupid enough to leave his seat belt unfastened, only about 8 percent of you buckle up.

A Smart Operator is a kid who knows the value of solitude. No one wants to be lonely, UNTR, but being alone can be an opportunity to look inward, think, plan, and better understand the world around you. It might help to keep a diary or journal. A famous French writer, Montaigne, said that he didn't know what he thought until he wrote it down. If that sounds crazy, try to find out what he meant by writing about your own feelings. You'll probably agree with him. At this moment, can you quickly answer a question like, What do you think of your mother? You can say one or two things, maybe, but it will take much longer, much more thought, much more patience to write down the whole story. And parts of it may surprise you. Which is what old Montaigne meant. Never be afraid to spend time with yourself.

A Pinhead is a kid who brags about her sex life. –6%! I've warned you about this in the chapter on sex, but I'm repeating it, repeating it, repeating it. It's stupid. It's a betrayal of the person you were with. It's wrong. It's not funny. It makes you look like a fool, even if your friends egg you on.

A Smart Operator is a kid who looks out for his siblings at school and in the neighborhood. No matter how much you think they embarrass or annoy you, UGTBK, because they're your responsibility. They share your genetic structure. Does that sound too heavy? It's the truth.

A Pinhead is a kid who whines, begs, and cajoles to get her way at home. UGTBK. Your parents don't deserve to have to deal with such behavior. You deserve better for yourself. You're on the way to adulthood, so it's time to learn that you cannot always get your way. There are better ways to get what you want. Learn them all. If you're ever tempted to act like this kind of pinhead, just make a recording of how you sound. You won't do it again.

A Smart Operator is a kid who stops and thinks. Take a timeout from your busy schedule, your socializing, your worrying, whatever . . . and look around you. Did you take the time to look up at Mars in 2003 when it was closer to Earth than it will ever be again in your lifetime? Do you know the names of the flowers in the garden next door? Do you know the home country of the couple who just opened a deli down the street? Look around. See where you are. So much in life exists only briefly. Catch it before it disappears.

A Pinhead is a kid who believes that horoscopes actually predict the future. They do not. Use your head. Have fun with them, if you like, but do not think that celestial objects billions of miles away are influencing your chances of getting a date for the prom or meeting Hilary Duff. YYSSLIBTO.

A Smart Operator is a kid who watches *The O'Reilly Factor* . . .

Ahem.

JJA.

No, my actual last i-message is this: kids at your age are funny, kind, resilient, curious, and a lot of other good things. For that reason, your parents and I don't want you to grow up quickly . . . but you will.

I hope this guide is helpful along the way, and I really appreciate your taking the time to read it. Just remember, life is tough, but it is also full of adventure and joy. Work hard, be honest, help others. Do those things, and you'll get the O'Reilly Guarantee: You will succeed! And I'll be happy when you do.

TTYL.

GLOSSARY
of IM TERMS

CMIIW: Correct me if I'm wrong

DEGT: Don't even go there

GAL: Get a life

GFI: Go for it

IDTS: I don't think so

IMHO: In my humble opinion

IMNSHO: In my not-so-humble opinion

IRMC: I rest my case

IYNWIM: If you know what I mean

JJA: Just joking again

Glossary of IM Terms

SMHID: Scratching my head in disbelief

SSINF: So stupid it's not funny

TTYL: Talk to you later

UGTBK: You got to be kidding

UNTR: U know that's right

YYSSLIBTO: Yeah, yeah, sure, sure, like I believe that one

-6%!: Not very clever

How you can get in touch with me

E-mail: oreilly@foxnews.com

Snail mail: Bill O'Reilly
c/o HarperCollins Publishers Inc.
10 East 53rd Street
9th Floor
New York, NY 10022-5299

.